大学生のためのコミュニケーション入門

Introduction to Communication for Japanese Students

ケビン・ヘファナン 著
Kevin Heffernan

Kurosio
くろしお出版

Preface

　私たちは生まれてからずっと、家族、友達、教師、愛するペットなど、周りの様々な人々や生き物と、日々コミュニケーションを行ってきました。その意味では、だれもがコミュニケーションの経験に富んでいると言えるでしょう。しかし、「コミュニケーションの仕組み」というのは、実際にはなかなか理解されていません。本書の目標は、コミュニケーションという現象を学問的にやさしく紹介することです。そのため、私は二つの要素を踏まえてこの本を書きました。一つ目は、自分自身が20年以上日本人と日本語で付き合ってきた個人的な経験、そして二つ目は、西欧の社会心理学の研究です。

　本書は主に二つのパートに分かれています。まず前半は、コミュニケーションに関する基本的な西欧理論の紹介です。よく知られている社会心理学の理論をいくつか選択し、私の個人的な観察や解釈を通して、日本の社会に適用することを試みています。紹介している研究は主に西欧圏で行われてきたものですが、それらの理論はコミュニケーションの基礎に関わるものであり、日本の文化にも適用することができると思います。例えば第2章で紹介する Social Identity Theory という理論は、文化に関わらず、どんな人にも適用することができます。

　後半のテーマは、(主に日本人と英語圏の人との間の) 異文化間コミュニケーションです。このパートでは、はじめに異文化間コミュニケーションの場面で会話が行き詰まりそうな談話、賛辞や謝罪の例などを紹介し、その次に、抽象的な異文化間コミュニケーション概念へと範囲を広げます。一例を

挙げると、なぜ英語の第一人称の「I」と違って、日本語では第一人称の言葉である「わたし」や「ぼく」が文法的に省略できるのかを、個人主義・集団主義の連続体関係という概念に沿って考える、といった内容です。

　本書は主に英語で執筆しています。コミュニケーションについて英語で書かれた教科書はすでに何冊かありますが、この本にはそれらと大きく違う点があります。それは、英語を第二言語として話す日本人大学生のニーズを考慮しているということです。また、難しい単語やスラング等については脚注で和訳・説明しているほか、日本語の例文もたくさん含まれています。そのため、英語がある程度理解できる（TOEFLで450点以上目安の）日本人大学生なら、あまり苦労せずに読むことができるでしょう。

　日本人同士のコミュニケーション、または異文化間コミュニケーションに興味を持つ人たちにとって、本書がその学びの入口になれば幸いです。

Kevin Heffernan

Contents

Part I: Introduction to Communication

1. Introduction ··1
    The building blocks of communication ································6
    Variation and context ··9
    A model of communication ···14
    Key points for Chapter 1 ··15
    Practice questions ··16
2. Categories, Prototypes, and Groups ·································18
    Categories ···18
    Prototypes ··24
    Categories, prototypes, and communication ·····················26
    Groups ··27
    Key points for Chapter 2 ··36
    Practice questions ··37
3. Audience Design and Communication Accommodation ··············40
    Audience design ···40
    Communication accommodation ·······································45
    Key points for Chapter 3 ··56
    Practice questions ··57

Part II: Intercultural Communication

4. Culture and Miscommunication ···60
    What is culture? ··60

    Surface culture and hidden culture ···63
    Gender, culture, and miscommunication ···68
    Key points for Chapter 4 ···74
    Practice questions ··75

5．Examples of Cultural Differences in Communication ················78
    Disagreement ··78
    Apologizing ···84
    Complimenting ···87
    Eye contact ···89
    Touching ···93
    Key points for Chapter 5 ···98
    Practice questions ··99

6．Culturally Dependent Communication Styles ··························103
    High context and low context styles ···103
    Group style and individual style communication ····························113
    Social power distance ···125
    Key points for Chapter 6 ···134
    Practice questions ··135

References ···139

1 Introduction

You communicate with other people every day—your family, your friends, your teacher, and even your pets. You have been communicating all of your life, and so you have lots of experience doing it. However, how well do you understand the communication process[1]? For example, can you answer the following question?

What is communication?

An obvious[2] answer to this question is something like the following. Communication is telling something to another person. For example, if I tell you, "Please close the window," then I am communicating with you. However, this answer is not enough. Let me give an example. We are sitting in a room at your house, the window is open, and it is getting a bit chilly[3]. I say to you, "It is getting cold in here," and you get up and close the window. I did not directly[4] tell you to close the window, and yet you did. I communicated the idea that "I would like the window closed" without using those words. So communication does not necessarily use words.

1　process: 過程，経過
2　obvious: 明らかな，見てすぐ分かる
3　chilly: 肌寒い
4　directly: 直接に

Consider the Japanese expression, 「空気を読む」. This expression describes communication without using words. Let us return to the question, "What is communication?" Now we have learned that it is sharing ideas and that it does not always require talking. Here is the definition of communication that we will use:

> Communication is the process of defining and sharing meaning.

This definition has two important parts: **defining meaning** (意味を定義する), and **sharing meaning** (意味を共有する). I will talk about these in turn.

■ Defining meaning

If I say to you, "Mimi ni mwalimu," are we communicating? These words mean "I am a teacher" in the Swahili language. Since you do not understand Swahili, you do not understand my message to you. Therefore, we are not communicating. You must understand the message in order to communicate. If we are using language to communicate, then we must understand the language. Language plays a very important role[5] in communication: it provides us with a set of words that we both understand. In other words, language defines the meaning of a set of words. For example, if we are communicating in Japanese, then the Japanese language defines the word 「大学」 to mean a "type of school." Defining meaning is the first step in communication.

Language is one way in which meaning is defined, but it is not the only way. Another way is through nonverbal[6] communication. For example, Japanese culture defines the action of pointing to your nose as having a specific[7] meaning, which is "myself." In contrast, pointing to your nose does

---

5   play a role: 役を演じる，役目を果たす
6   nonverbal: 非言語
7   specific: 特定の

not have this meaning in Western culture. This is just one example of a culturally-defined meaning. There are many others.

Culture (including both language and nonverbal communication) is our main source of meaning definitions. However, many living organisms[8] do not have culture, and yet they are still able to communicate. For example, bees communicate the distance and direction to a source of food by performing a complex[9] "waggle dance". A waggle dance consists of[10] flying in a wavy-line[11] pattern for a short distance and at a certain angle. The distance and angle of the flight path communicate the distance and direction to the food source. The bee repeats the waggle dance over and over, and in this way communicates with other bees. The bee does not learn the "language" of the waggle dance by taking dance lessons. Rather, the definition of the meaning is in the bee's genes[12]. Meaning definitions are part of the genes of all living organisms, not only bees.

I will give another example of communication without culture, this time from the world of plants. Some plants can communicate with animals and insects. One example of this is the lima bean plant. The lima bean plant is a favorite food of the spider mite[13], a tiny insect that eats leaves. When the lima bean plant is attacked by spider mites, the plant releases a chemical in to the air. This chemical attracts[14] other insects that like to eat spider mites. These other insects attack the spider mites, preventing the spider mites from eating the lima bean plant.

---

8 organism: 生物体
9 complex: 複雑な
10 consist of: 〜から成り立つ
11 wavy: 起伏が多い，波状の；from the noun wave
12 gene: 遺伝子
13 mite: ダニの種類
14 attract: 引き付ける，引き寄せる

In summary[15], defining meaning is the first step in communication. Without a common[16] understanding of a specific meaning, communication cannot take place, as we saw in the Swahili example. Most of our communication uses language, a set of words and phrases with defined meanings. However, language is only one part of culture. Nonverbal communication also consists of many definitions of meaning, such as the example of pointing to your nose. Finally, language and culture are not the only sources of meaning definitions. They are also found in the genes of all living organisms—insects, plants, bacteria[17], and humans.

■ Sharing meaning

The second step in communication is sharing meaning. Sharing meaning is the process of sending a message from sender to receiver. At least two separate organisms must be involved for sharing to take place. Returning to the example in which I asked you to close the window, the sharing takes place by talking. I am the sender and you are the receiver.

Talking is only one of many ways in which communication takes place, but our definition of communication is not limited to talking. In the previous example that I gave of a bee communicating the location of food, the sharing of meaning occurs through the bee's motion[18]. In the example of the lima bean, however, the communication takes place through a chemical that is released in to the air.

The key ingredients[19] to our definition of communication are two or more organisms, and something (such as language or a chemical) that has

---

15　in summary: 要約すると
16　common: 共有の
17　bacteria: ばい菌
18　motion: 動き
19　ingredient: 要素

a common meaning among them. In the case of human speech, words have a common meaning between the speaker and the listener. In the case of the bee waggle dance, the motions have a common meaning between the bees. In the case of the lima bean plant, the chemical has common meaning between the plant and the insects that it attracts.

The main focus of this book is verbal communication. Nonverbal, culturally-based communication such as hand gestures will also be discussed[20]. Communication that is not based on culture, such as the communication between bees or the communication between plants, animals and insects is not discussed further. From this point on, the discussion focuses on communication between humans.

In the remainder of this chapter, several key ideas and words are introduced. These ideas and words make the foundation for the topics covered in the remaining chapters. At the end of this chapter, these ideas are presented[21] in a simple diagram[22] that illustrates[23] the model of communication introduced in this chapter.

> Check your understanding 1.1
> Fireflies are insects that can emit[24] light from their bodies. They use patterns of light to attract mates[25]. Is this communication?
> *Answer: Yes, it is communication. The emitted light has a defined meaning—I want a mate. There are two or more organisms involved, so the meaning is being shared. Therefore this is communication.*

---

20 discuss: 話題にする；related to the noun *discussion*
21 present: a formal way to say "show"; related to the noun *presentation*
22 diagram: 図，略図
23 illustrate: 実例や図解を使って説明する
24 emit: 出す，放つ
25 mate: 動物の配偶者

The building blocks of communication

In this section, I introduce the building blocks of communication. Communication requires at least three components[26]: a speaker, a message, and an addressee[27]. The **speaker** is the person who is sending the message. Most often, this is the person speaking, as suggested by the word "speaker". However, communication does not require talking. The next section explains more about this. The **message** is the idea being communicated. The **addressee** is the person who is the target of the message.

■ The parts of a message

As mentioned[28], the main focus of this book is verbal communication. However, verbal communication is only one component of a message. Consider the following message: "You're late!" I could say this with an angry tone of voice[29]. I could also say this by whispering[30] and smiling. I might say this message as if I was asking a question and while poking[31] you in the stomach. These examples include both verbal and nonverbal communication, and both are important. The message changes depending on my tone of voice and my gestures, from "I am angry that you are late," to "you think you are late, but really you are not late."

Nonverbal communication is further divided into two types: a nonverbal

---

26 component: 構成要素をなす部分
27 address: 話しかける，呼びかける
    addressee: 話しかけられる人
28 as mentioned: 前述したように
29 tone of voice: 声の調子
30 whisper: ささやく
31 poke: 指でさす

component and a paralinguistic component (The difference between these is explained below). Altogether, a message consists of three components:

1. verbal component （言語）
2. nonverbal component （非言語）⎫ nonverbal
3. paralinguistic component （パラ言語）⎭ communication

The receiver of a message uses all three components to understand the full meaning of a message.

Verbal component

The **verbal component** is the actual words spoken by the speaker. In the above example, this would be the words "You're late!".

Nonverbal component

The **nonverbal component** is not spoken, but it is still suggested. An easy way to understand this is to think of the verbal component as 建前 and the nonverbal component as 本音. Most of the time, the verbal component and the nonverbal component overlap[32], but not always. For example, upon meeting a new person, Japanese people sometimes say, 「遊びに来てください」. However, they do not necessarily want that person to come over to their house; this is simply a polite phrase[33] to say when you meet someone for the first time (Elwood 2001). Perhaps later they will really want that person to come and visit. If so, this will be made clear with further invitations, choosing a time, and so on. In the case of the polite expression, the verbal component is "Please come and visit," but the nonverbal component is "I am just being polite."

Here is another example. You come home from school late in the

---

32 overlap: 重複する
33 In Japanese, polite phrases such as this one are called 社交辞令.

evening, and your mother says to you, "There is food in the refrigerator." The verbal component of this message tells you nothing new, as you already know that if you open the door to the refrigerator, you will see food. Why, then, is your mother telling you this? This message has a nonverbal component as well, which is "If you are hungry, open up the refrigerator, take out the leftover food from dinner, and eat it." In this example, the verbal component and the nonverbal component are different.

Paralinguistic component

The **paralinguistic component** consists of the facial[34] expressions, hand gestures, tone of voice, etc., that accompany[35] the message. The prefix[36] *para-* means alongside, or side-by-side. Some other English words that use this prefix are *parallel* (to be side-by-side), *paragraph* (historically, this word meant little marks written alongside the text), and *paramedic* (a person who works alongside a doctor). The paralinguistic component is the gestures, and so on, that accompany the words. The paralinguistic component provides very important clues for understanding the nonverbal component.

Check your understanding 1.2
A person smiles at another person to show that he is happy. What is the verbal component? What is the nonverbal component? What is the paralinguistic component?
Answer: Because nothing is spoken, there is no verbal component. The nonverbal component is the feelings being expressed—happiness. The paralinguistic component is the facial expression—the smile.

---

34   facial: 表面の
35   accompany: 伴う，同時に起きる
36   prefix: 接頭辞

Introduction

Variation and context[37]

In the previous section, communication was defined as a two-step process. In the first step, meaning is defined. In the second step, meaning is shared. One characteristic of communication is that there are many ways to share the same meaning. Consider the question, "Have you already eaten?" How do you say this in Japanese?

There is more than one way to say this sentence in Japanese:
- ご飯はもう食べましたか。
- ご飯はもう食べた？
- すでに召し上がりましたか。
- 飯食った？

■ Variants

Each of these ways of saying "Have you already eaten?" is called a **variant** (変異形), and together they are called **variation**. Thus, the same expression has multiple variants. Likewise, communication has variation.

Although each of the variants in the above example can be translated into the same English phrase, "Have you eaten yet?" to a Japanese speaker, 「飯食った？」 is very different from 「ご飯はもう食べましたか」. The first expression is informal[38], and is only used with friends and family members. The second expression is much more formal[39], and is used with people you do not know very well, or people who are higher in social status[40]. Thus, a Japanese speaker knows that these phrases contain much more meaning

---

37 context: コンテクスト，文脈
38 informal: 砕けた
39 formal: 改まった，硬い
40 social status: 社会的地位

than "Have you already eaten?"

Some variants are variation between formal and informal language, as seen in the above example. Another source of variation is dialect[41]. Following is a list of Japanese dialect variants for the word snail:

- かたつむり
- でんでんむし
- かだつぶり
- まいまい
- めめんじょ

Other ways that words with the same meaning can vary are masculine[42] and feminine[43] language (for example, おれ versus うち), and older language and newer language (for example, お母さん versus ママ).

■ Context

The meaning of a variant depends on the **context** of communication. It would not be polite to use the phrase 「飯食った？」with a professor. In a similar way, using the phrase 「ご飯はもう食べましたか」with your younger brother is also strange. You choose your words depending on who you are talking to. The person you are talking to is part of the context. **Context** is the environment in which the communication takes place, and it determines which variant to use.

> Context determines which variant to use.

Context is determined by several different aspects[44] of communication, not only the person you are talking to. Following is a list of the parts of

---

41 dialect: 方言
42 masculine: 男らしい
43 feminine: 女らしい
44 aspect: 物事の一つの面，様相

context that I talk about in this book:
- personal characteristics of the speaker
- the personal characteristics of the addressee
- relationship between the speaker and the addressee
- the situation
- culture

Personal characteristics of the speaker
As you speak, your speech shows your personality. If you want to show that you are tough or masculine, you may often use words such as「てめぇ」,「ぬかす」and「しやがる」. If you are elderly, you probably do not use recent fashionable words such as「草食系男子」and「アラフォー」. Likewise[45], if you are young, you most likely make very frequent[46] use of the word「なんか」, as well as other new words such as「フォロー」and「合コン」. Finally, if you are from the Kansai area, then you probably say the word「雨」differently from people who are from the Kanto area.

A person's speech shows many characteristics of the speaker, such as age, gender, and where he or she grew up. A different way of looking at this is that you adjust[47] your speech to match your personal characteristics by frequently using some words while avoiding others. In this way, you, as the speaker, are part of the context of communication.

Personal characteristics of the addressee
Similar to the way you adjust your speech to match your characteristics, you also adjust your speech to match the addressee's characteristics. For example, university students use a lot more loanwords[48] when talking to

---

45 likewise: 同じく，同様に
46 frequent: 頻繁な
47 adjust: 調節する

other university students than when talking to their parents or grandparents (Hogan 2003). Following are some examples of loanwords used among university students:
- プラスアルファ
- フレンドリー
- インターナショナル
- アクティブ
- シューズ

In this way, university students adjust how often they use loanwords in their speech to match whom they are talking to.

Other examples of the ways in which you adjust your speech are:
- rude / polite speech（ぬかす versus おっしゃる）
- masculine / feminine speech（俺 versus あたし）
- dialect / standard language（もうええんちゃう？ versus もういいんじゃない？）

You must frequently adjust your speech to match the characteristics of the addressee, such as friendship level, age, and gender. If you begin talking to a different person, then your speech changes to match the characteristics of that person. The addressee is a very important part of the context.

The relationship between the speaker and the addressee

The relationship between the speaker and the addressee is another important part of the context. You speak in a friendly, casual style（タメ口）with your grandmother, but in a polite style（敬語）with a friend of your grandmother, although both people have similar characteristics. You change your style of speech to match your relationship. Your relationship to your grandmother is "family member," whereas your relationship with your grandmother's friend is more distant. Similarly, you speak politely to

---

48 loanword: 外来語

your boss, to your teachers, and to strangers, but speak in a more casual style with friends, classmates, and siblings[49].

The situation

You adjust your speech depending on the situation. You speak in standard Japanese when you are giving a presentation to your classmates, but use dialect when you are eating lunch with those same classmates.

Culture

The last component of context is culture. You adjust your message to match the culture you are in. For example, in Western culture, it is important to look at someone's eyes while talking. If you do not, it suggests that you are lying or are embarrassed. This is very different from Japanese culture. The role of culture is discussed in detail in the second half of this book, which focuses on intercultural communication[50] between Japanese and non-Japanese speakers.

> Check your understanding 1.3
> Match the expressions on the left with the contexts on the right.
> a. はじめまして　　　　1. You are giving a formal presentation
> b. 君、大丈夫か　　　　2. A male teenager is talking to a close friend
> c. ご清聴を感謝します　3. You are meeting a person for the first time
> d. おめぇがばかや！　　4. You are talking to a 後輩
> *Answers: a-3; b-4; c-1; d-2*

---

49 sibling: 兄弟
50 intercultural communication: 異文化間コミュニケーション

A model of communication

Figure 1.1 presents a simple model of communication. The diagram shows How a message is communicated from a speaker to an addressee. The message consists of three components: verbal, nonverbal and paralinguistic. The message is influenced by the context.

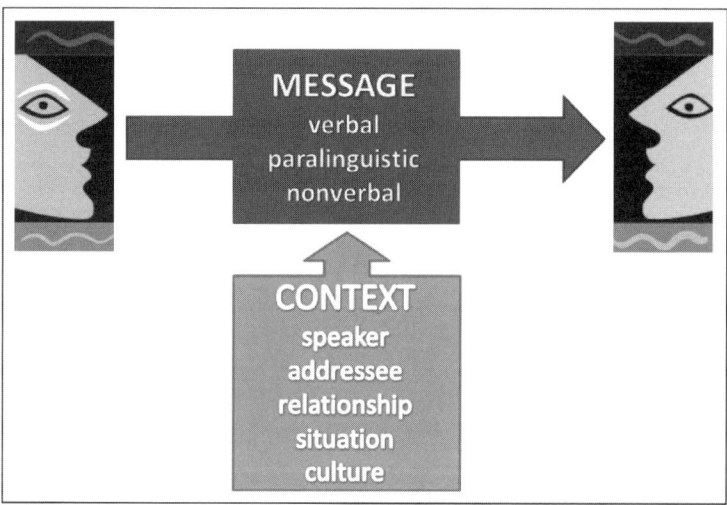

Figure 1.1: A simple model of communication

Introduction

Key points for Chapter 1

▶ Communication is a two-step process:
   1. defining meaning
   2. sharing meaning
▶ Verbal meaning (the meaning of words such as 犬) is defined by language. Nonverbal meaning (for example, the meaning of the gesture pointing to your nose) is defined by culture.
▶ Communication involves a speaker, a message, and an addressee. The message consists of three components: the verbal message, the nonverbal message and the paralinguistic message.
▶ When you share meaning, you adjust the message to match the context. Following is the list of context talked about in this chapter, along with examples.
   - personal characteristics of the speaker (ex., gender of speaker)
   - personal characteristics of the addressee (ex., age of addressee)
   - relationship between the speaker and the addressee (ex., close friends)
   - situation (ex., job interview)
   - culture (ex., Japanese culture)

PRACTICE QUESTIONS

Q 1.1 Sometimes students fall asleep in class. According to the definition given in this book, is this communication? Why or why not?

Q 1.2 For each of the following examples of communication, explain what the meaning of the message is, and how that meaning is being shared.
- a peacock[51] spreading out its tail feathers in order to attract a mate
- clapping[52] your hands repeatedly
- a dog urinating[53] on a tree to indicate its territory

Q 1.3 The word "I" in Japanese has many variants, such as「おれ」and「じぶん」. List five Japanese variants for the word "I" and circle the variant that you use the most often.

Q 1.4 Read the following Japanese and then guess the answers to these questions. Is the speaker a Japanese person? How old is the speaker? Where is the speaker from? Is the speaker male or female?

それを持ってボランティアができてんねん。ほんで、シルバー人材センターで友達ぎょうさんできたん。60過ぎてから。ほんで、もうしょっちゅう飲みに行ってる。友達、物凄いできたん。

Q 1.5 There are foreign Christian missionaries[54] living in Japan. Their

---
51 peacock: 雄のクジャク
52 clap hands: 拍手する
53 urinate: 放尿する
54 Christian missionary: キリスト教宣教師

Introduction

mission is to spread the Christian religion among the Japanese people. One way they do this is by walking along the streets and visiting houses one-by-one. In Japan, many people are of the Buddhist faith[55]. Sometimes, such people do not want to talk to Christian missionaries. After a Christian missionary introduces himself in Japanese, the Japanese person may give a response such as 「英語ができません」, hoping that the missionary will go away. Of course, the missionary is speaking Japanese, so even if the Japanese person cannot speak English, that does not matter[56]. However, there is a very important nonverbal component to the message 「英語ができません」. What is it?

Q 1.6 Turn to page 83 and read the Japanese story about the young man. For the phrase 「考えさせて下さい」, fill in the following information:

speaker:	_____
addressee:	_____
relationship:	_____
verbal message:	考えさせて下さい
nonverbal message:	_____

---

55 faith: 信仰
56 does not matter: 関係がない

2 Categories, Prototypes, and Groups

This chapter examines how people view the world. The ideas presented here are important to our understanding of the communication process. People who view the world differently communicate with the world around them differently. The chapter begins by introducing the idea of a category.

Categories

Psychology research has shown that people view the world as categories[1] (Geeraerts 2006). They see something and subconsciously[2] assign[3] it to a category. A **category** is a collection of examples of similar phenomena, objects, ideas, and so on, with a single label. For example, when you see a poodle, you assign the animal to the category with the label of DOG. You make this decision based on your knowledge of the characteristics of dogs (they bark[4], walk on four legs, have fur), and the characteristics of the poodle (it barks, walks on four legs, has fur). You then naturally think that

---

1 category: カテゴリー
2 subconsciously: 無意識的に
3 assign: 割り当てる
4 bark: 吠える

the poodle is a dog, and you use your knowledge of dogs when you interact[5] with the poodle. Of course, the poodle is a dog, and so your interactions are likely to be successful.

The categorization process is important to communication. In order to understand this process, let us first talk more about it in general. How do humans learn this process? Is it something that we learn as we grow up, like our language? Perhaps it is more like our ability to see. We do not learn to see; seeing is automatic. Research has shown that categorization is a combination of the two: Some parts of the process are inherent[6] to being human, while other parts are learned from the culture we grow up in.

■ Categorization of colors

I just stated[7] that the categorization process is a combination of cultural and inherent knowledge. This combination is seen in the words for colors. Every language of the world has words for dark and light colors, and people, regardless of culture, tend to categorize light and dark colors the same way. Look at the four shades[8] of gray in Figure 2.1. Which of the squares are dark and which are light?

Figure 2.1: Which of these are light colors and which are dark colors?

---

5 interact: 交流する
6 inherent: 固有の；本来備わっている，生まれつきの
7 state: 述べる
8 shade (of a color): 色合い

Almost everyone responds with the same answer: light, dark, dark, light. Determining whether a color is light or dark does not depend on culture. Rather, the ability to make this decision seems to be universal (that is, every human can do it). But what about colors other than gray, such as red, yellow, green, and blue? Are all colors universal?

In fact, people view colors differently. Furthermore, there are large differences between languages of the world (Berlin & Kay 1969). For example, consider the list of color words in Table 2.1 from the language Tiv, spoken in Nigeria, Africa. Tiv uses only three words, one word for dark colors, one word for light colors, and one word for colors that are similar to yellow, orange, red, and brown.

Tiv	English Translation
pupu	light blue, light green, light gray, white
ii	dark blue, dark green, dark gray, black
nyian	brown, red, orange, yellow

Table 2.1: Tiv color words and their English translations (from Berlin & Kay 1969)

In the 1960s, several anthropologists[9] travelled the world gathering data on color words from many languages of the world. They discovered that some color words, such as the word *red*, were very common, while other words such as *pink* were much rarer (Berlin & Kay 1969). That is, many languages of the world have a word for red, but few languages have a word for pink. Furthermore, they found that there was a hierarchy[10] of color words. The color words were ranked[11] in the following order:

1. black, white

---

9   anthropologist: 人類学者
10 hierarchy: 階級制
11 rank: 順位をつける

2. red
3. blue, yellow, green
4. brown
5. purple, pink, orange, gray

Languages that have words from the higher-numbered ranks, such as *brown* and *pink*, tended to have words from the lower-numbered ranks, such as *red* and *black*. However, the reverse is not true; the researchers found many languages that had words from the lower-numbered ranks, but did not have words from the higher-numbered ranks. In other words[12], the color words are like building a tower; you must first have the lower words before you can add the higher words. The lower words form the foundation for the higher words.

This pattern of ranking color words is surprisingly consistent[13] from one language to the next. This suggests an inherent quality to this ranking process that is independent of culture, and this is evidence that color categories are inherent human knowledge. However, the actual culture itself determines which words are included in the language, and thus color words are a combination of inherent knowledge and cultural knowledge.

■ Color words in Chinese, Japanese, and English

It may seem that languages such as Chinese, Japanese, and English do not truly fit this pattern. These languages have words for all of these colors. However, if we look more closely, there are interesting patterns. Table 2.2 lists the Chinese and Japanese words for colors, divided up in to the five steps of the color hierarchy.

Table 2.2 shows some trends. In the case of the Chinese words, those

---

12 in other words: 換言すれば，すなわち
13 consistent: 一貫している

words in the lower ranks use only one Chinese character[14], while those words in the higher ranks use two Chinese characters. Therefore, the Chinese color words show a pattern that fit the hierarchy of color words.

Rank	Chinese	Japanese
One	黒　白	黒い　白い
Two	紅	赤い
Three	緑　黄色　藍色	緑　青い 黄色い　黄色
Four	茶色	茶色い　茶色
Five	紫紅色　桃色 橙色　灰色	紫　ピンク 灰色　オレンジ

Table 2.2: Color words in Chinese and Japanese

Does Japanese also show a pattern that fits the hierarchy of color words? The words in the lower ranks tend to be 形容詞, whereas the words in the higher ranks tend to be 形容動詞. Furthermore, the words in the middle ranks tend to be both 形容詞 and 形容動詞. Finally, *katakana* loanwords are only in the highest rank.

These patterns suggest that the words in the lower ranks are more native-like[15] or central to the languages. In general, 形容詞 tend to be old Japanese words, whereas 形容動詞 tend to be loanwords, borrowed first from Chinese about 1500 to 1000 years ago, and more recently from English over the last 150 years. Thus we see the Japanese color words fit the color hierarchy very well; the older words are all lower-ranked words, while the higher-ranked words are all more recent additions to the language.

English shows a similar pattern. The history of the words[16] shows that

---

14　Chinese character: 漢字

15　native-like: 先天的な，固有の

16　The history of an English word can be checked using the *Oxford English Dictionary*.

the lower-ranked English color words such as *black, white*, and *red* are all very old words that were in the English language before the first written records. In contrast, the higher-ranking words such as brown and purple are loanwords and were introduced into the English language approximately 700 years ago. The word *pink* is the youngest, and was introduced into the English language about 500 years ago.

The consistency[17] of ranking colors across many different languages strongly suggests that the ranks are connected to the human brain, and that the order of the ranks is independent of culture and language. However, which colors are in a language is of course dependent on the language. These examples using words for colors illustrate the following point: Categorization is both (1) inherent knowledge and (2) dependent on the culture and language a person learns growing up.

Check your understanding 2.1

English has several words for colors that belong[18] to the category RED, such as *crimson, scarlet, cardinal*, and *maroon*. How many different Japanese words can you think of that belong to the category RED? Two examples are 赤 and 紅. Can you think of at least two more?

Answer: 朱 , 丹

A researcher is recording a newly-discovered language. She learns the words for *red, green, black*, and *brown*, but she is not sure if there are words for other colors. Do you think there are probably words for *white, yellow*, and *pink*?

Answer: There are probably words for white and yellow, because these colors are lower in rank than brown. However, there may not be a word for pink because it is higher in rank than brown.

---

17 consistency: 一貫性
18 belong: 所属する

■ An example of a category: Seaweed

I will end this section with a simple example of the way categories are determined by culture. As I stated, a category is a collection of similar objects or ideas. One example of a category is SEAWEED. Every language in the world has words for plants, and those cultures that are located near the ocean most likely have words for plants that grow in the ocean, such as the English word *seaweed*. Depending on the culture, some languages have several different categories of seaweed. One example is the Japanese language. Table 2.3 shows the different Japanese and English words for categories and subcategories of ocean plants. As this table shows, there are two categories for seaweed in the Japanese language, whereas there is only one category in the English language. The difference is because categories are determined by cultural knowledge as well as inherent knowledge.

	Categories	Examples
Japanese	海草	あまも、すがも
	海藻	こんぶ、わかめ、もずく
English	seaweed	*seaweed*

Table 2.3: Examples of the categories for seaweed in English and Japanese

Prototypes

In the previous section, I introduced the idea of a category. I defined[19] a category as a collection of examples of similar objects, ideas, phenomena, and so on. Every category also has a prototype[20]. A **prototype** is an

---

19 define: 定義する
20 prototype: an approximate Japanese translation is 典型

abstract[21] example of a category that includes all of the most common characteristics of the examples in that category. For example, consider the category of BIRD. The prototype for the BIRD category includes the following characteristics:
- has wings
- can fly
- lays eggs
- sings a bird song
- lives in trees
- eats insects
- is a warm-blooded animal[22]

Many birds have most of these characteristics. Such birds are **prototypical**, that is, they closely fit the prototype. However, some birds do not fit the prototype, such as penguins and ostriches[23]. Such birds are **non-prototypical**.

Research on prototypes has shown us that humans use prototypes when they think (Rosch 1975; Geeraerts 2006). For example, when shown pictures of different objects and then asked questions about them, people responded faster to questions about prototypical objects. Similarly, when asked to give examples of things from a category, people tended to list only the prototypical examples from the category. To illustrate this, perform[24] the following exercise. Quickly decide which of the following items are fruits, and which are vegetables:
- りんご
- バナナ

21　abstract: 抽象的な
22　warm-blooded animal: 温血動物
23　ostrich: ダチョウ
24　perform: 遂行する

- トマト
- かぼちゃ

As you performed the exercise, you most likely found that りんご was very easy to classify, but かぼちゃ was more difficult. Why is this? This is because りんご is more prototypical than かぼちゃ (i.e., has more of the characteristics of the category FRUIT), and prototypical examples are easier to classify[25].

> **Check your understanding 2.2**
> List three characteristics for a prototypical JAPANESE PERSON.
> *Answer: Speaks Japanese; eats fish; lives for a long time; (other answers are also possible)*

Categories, prototypes, and communication

When you first meet a person, you assign him to various categories. You also assume that this new person is a prototype, that is, a prototypical member of the categories to which you have assigned him (Hogg 2006: 118). For example, if you meet a female person from Japan, then you assume[26] that she is a prototypical Japanese, and that she is prototypical woman. You know the characteristics of a prototypical Japanese person and a prototypical woman; therefore, you assume your new friend has these characteristics. For example, you know that a prototypical Japanese person speaks the Japanese language fluently, and you know that women tend to not use profanity[27] when they talk. Thus, you assume that your new

---

25 classify: 分類する
26 assume: 証拠はないが当然のことと決めてかかる，仮定する；the noun is *assumption*

friend speaks Japanese and does not use bad language very often.

Now suppose that the person that you just met is not Japanese, but is a foreigner. Furthermore, suppose she is Caucasian[28]. Now you assign her to the category WESTERNER, and assume that she is a prototypical Westerner. Two of the characteristics of a prototypical Westerner are that they speak English, and that they do not speak Japanese very well. Thus, you assume that your new friend can speak English, but cannot speak Japanese.

It is important to understand that your assumptions are based on the characteristics of prototypical members of a category, but not all members are prototypical. That is, your assumptions are often very wrong. Perhaps your friend is Russian, and does not speak English very well, or perhaps your friend is Caucasian but was born in Japan, and speaks Japanese as a native language. As you learn this new information, you adjust your communication style to match the individual and not the prototype. For example, if you learn that the person you just met speaks Japanese fluently, you will speak in Japanese with her.

Groups

The previous sections talked about how a person is assigned to a category, and how we assume that person has the prototypical characteristics of that category. For example, if you met a Japanese person while travelling in the United States, you would assume that the person likes to eat raw fish because this is one of the characteristics of a prototypical Japanese person.

When we talk about people, rather than animals or objects, we normally

---

27 profanity: 冒とく, 罵り言葉
28 Caucasian: a polite way of saying 白人

do not use the word category. Instead, we use the word "group." A **group** is a collection of people from the same category. For example, everyone who attends the same university is a part of group. Similarly, everyone from the Kansai area of Japan is a part of a group.

Every person belongs to several groups. The groups to which you belong vary[29] from specific[30] to general. An example of a specific group to which you belong is your small group of close friends. An example of a general group that you belong to is the Japanese population.

Recall[31] that when you meet a new person, you assign her to a category, or a group. Furthermore, a distinction[32] is made between in-group and out-group (Triandis 1994). **In-groups** are groups to which you also belong. **Out-groups** are groups to which you do not belong. Thus, if you meet Japanese student from a different university, you assign her to the in-group of JAPANESE UNIVERSITY STUDENT, and to the out-group of DIFFERENT UNIVERSITY.

Social psychologists have researched how people from different groups interact with each other. Their observations[33] have been gathered as a theory of social psychology called the *Social Identity Theory* (see Hogg 2006). This research has revealed[34] several key points about communication:

- people tend to compare groups to each other in order to decide which group is better
- people are bias[35] towards members of in-groups, and bias against members of out

---

29 vary: 変化する
30 specific: 具体的な，詳細な
31 recall: 思い出す
32 distinction: 区別，識別
33 observation: 観測，観察
34 reveal: 明かす

-groups
- people want the in-groups and the out-groups to be different
- people want the in-group to be better

The common theme here is comparing groups and deciding that your group is better.

Comparing groups seems to be a natural part of interacting with other people. When groups are compared, our bias towards our own groups causes us to believe that our group is better (Tajfel & Turner 1979, Turner et al. 1979). For example, when you meet students from other universities, you naturally and subconsciously compare their university to your own, and tend to believe that the university you attend is better.

As part of this comparison[36] process, people look for and exaggerate[37] differences between groups. Similarly, people overlook and play down[38] similarities (Turner 1975). For example, perhaps your university has a 史跡同好会 and another university does not. Visiting historical ruins[39] is not a popular activity among university students, and most likely you would never join such a club. Nevertheless, this difference will seem like a great reason to attend your university. This is in spite[40] of all of the clubs that are at both universities, such as 野球部 and 軽音楽部. This emphasis[41] on difference is important because people want their in-groups to be noticeably[42]

---

35 bias: 偏見を持つ，偏る
    bias towards A: Aの都合がいいように事情を解釈する
    bias against B: Bの都合が悪いように事情を解釈する
36 comparison: 比較
37 exaggerate: 誇張する，大げさに言う
38 play down: 軽視する，みくびる
39 historical ruins: 史跡
40 in spite of: にもかかわらず，物ともせず
41 emphasis: 重要視
42 noticeably: 目立つように，顕著に

different from out-groups. These differences create a strong sense of identity and a sense of belonging[43] among group members.

As previously stated, people also want their in-groups to be superior[44]. This is particularly true in organized[45] competition, such as competitive sports. If your group does well, then your self-esteem[46] rises. Note that you do not need to participate in the competition yourself; you just need to identify yourself as a member of the group that is competing. For example, one of the professional baseball teams in Japan is the Hanshin Tigers. This team is not known for being a very strong team, but it certainly has very enthusiastic[47] fans. Hanshin Tigers' fans identify themselves as members of a group, and when the baseball team wins, the self-esteem of the fans also rises. Fans enthusiastically compare their team to other teams, and often conclude that their team is the best. If the team does not do well, then the biased fans conclude that the team was simply unlucky, not that the team is bad.

Check your understanding 2.3
You belong to several different groups, such as your family and your university. Make a list of three more groups to which you belong.

■ A detailed example: The groups 内 and 外

Cultures across the world are quite different. For example, Japanese culture makes a clear distinction between 内 and 外 (Elwood 2001, 賀川洋 1997). These are two groups, and we can think of characteristics of

---

43 sense of belonging: 親近感
44 superior: 優れる
45 organized: 組織的な；example: *organized crime* 組織犯罪
46 self-esteem: 自尊心
47 enthusiastic: 熱心な

prototypical members in each of them. Here are some of the characteristics of a prototypical member of the 内 group:
- related by family or belongs to the same group as you (company, club, team, and so on)
- speaks タメ口 with you
- same social rank as you (i.e., not your boss)

Here are some of the characteristics of a prototypical member of the 外 group:
- a person (either Japanese or foreigner)
- not related by family and does belong to the same group
- speaks 敬語 with you

It is important to remember that not every member of a group has every characteristic. Furthermore, these lists are just some of the typical characteristics. I am sure you can think of other characteristics of a prototypical member of the above groups.

Now that we have a good idea of the group, we can think of some examples of both prototypical and non-prototypical members of each group. Some prototypical members of the 内 group are *your brother, your best friend, your colleague*[48], and *your classmate*. Some prototypical members of the 外 group are *a stranger, your boyfriend's mother*, and *your teacher*.

Each of these group also has non-prototypical members. A non-prototypical member has one or more different characteristics from those listed above. For example, consider the characteristic of *person* for the 内 group. A member of this group that is not a person is your dog. You treat your dog as a family member, and speak タメ口 with it. Your dog is a non-prototypical member of the 内 group. What about the 外 group? We can

---

48 colleague: 同僚

again use the idea that a non-prototypical member is not human, and give the example of a 1500-year-old tree. Japanese have great respect for such trees, and it is reasonable to imagine a caretaker[49] talking to the tree. If so, perhaps the caretaker would treat the tree as a member of the 外 group and use 敬語. The tree is a non-prototypical member of the 外 group.

Now look again at the model of communication presented at the end of the last chapter (page 14). The context consists of several parts. The parts of the context that are being discussed here are the *addressee*, and the *relationship* between the speaker and the addressee. We have just learned about that the group, or category, that the addressee belongs to, and the characteristics of those categories influences communication. For example, if the addressee is a dog, you will probably not use 敬語. How realistic is the following conversation?

   コロちゃん：　ワン、ワン！
    飼い主：　はい、かしこまりました。

It is not very realistic. Most dog owners use ため口 with their pets.

■ The example of Yuna Kim

This section presents an example of groups that comes from the 2010 Winter Olympics. The ladies singles figure skating competition was won by a Korean named Yuna Kim（金妍兒）. Kim's performance was considered outstanding, and she set two world records during the Olympics. She was praised by people throughout the world. For example, Hilary Clinton, the Secretary of State for the United States, described Kim's performance as extraordinary[50, 51].

---

49 caretaker: 管理人
50 extraordinary: 非凡な，顕著な
51 Hwang, Doo-hyong. Feb. 27, 2010. Clinton lauds Kim Yu-na for magnificent performance. *Yonhap News*. Retrieved August 8, 2011.

In spite of such international praise, some Japanese criticized[52] her. Kim has been a rival[53] of Japanese skaters for the past five years, particularly that of Mao Asada（浅田真央）(Strange et al. 2011: 813). Between 2005 and 2009, Kim placed first and a Japanese competitor placed second a total of nine times. In the Olympics, Kim once again place first while Asada placed second.

Immediately after the event, the competition was a popular topic of discussion on blogs such as 2ちゃんねる[54]. For the most part, comments about Kim were negative, while comments about Asada were positive. Following are some examples of comments about Kim taken from 2ちゃんねる：

- 真央ちゃんの演技好きだけど今回は安藤美姫さんとキムヨナの演技の方が、良かったと思った。
- 日本の選手以外の選手も素晴らしい演技を見ると感動しましたが、キムヨナの演技は上手と思うけど感動はしない。
- 彼女を見ると不快感を感じます。

The people who posted these comments acknowledged[55] Kim's technical ability, but still criticized her. This is an excellent example of the *Social Identity Theory*. Japanese people naturally identify themselves as a single group that includes Japanese skaters such as Mao Asada, and they identify Koreans as an out-group, which would include Yuna Kim. These two groups are compared, and because people tend to be biased against an out-group, Japanese people are biased against Kim even though she gave an outstanding performance. The motivation behind bias against an out-group

---

52　criticize: 非難する；the noun form is *criticism*
53　rival: 敵手
54　2ちゃんねる：http://www2.2ch.net/2ch2.html
55　acknowledge: 認める

is a desire[56] for the in-group to be better than out-group. In the 2010 Winter Olympics, the Japanese skaters were unable to beat Yuna Kim technically, but according to these comments, the performances were more enjoyable to watch. Thus, in this way, the in-group can still feel that their group is superior, and self-esteem is raised.

Such negative attitudes towards an out-group, particularly when competition is involved, are natural and very common. Ask any passionate[57] sports fan anywhere in the world about his favorite team, and he will most likely have something positive to say about his team, and something negative to say about the other teams and their fans. For example, during an American League Championship Series, the CEO of the baseball team the Texas Rangers commented in an interview[58] that New York Yankees' fans are "violent, apathetic[59] and an embarrassment". In contrast, he described Texas Rangers' fans as "great". Here again we see the pattern of a person being biased towards an in-group and being biased against an out-group.

Such bias is perhaps forgivable[60] in our daily lives. After all, a natural part of conversation with other members of our in-group is criticism of out-groups. These criticisms are an important tool for building the self-esteem of the in-group members. However, there are many situations in which we must be aware of[61] and eliminate[62] our bias against out-groups. Such situations include competitive sports judges, intercultural communication,

---

56 desire: 欲望
57 passionate: 情熱的な
58 ESPN: http://sports.espn.go.com/mlb/playoffs/2010/news/story?id=5752715. Retrieved Sept. 1, 2011.
59 apathetic: 無関心
60 forgivable: 許される
61 be aware of: 意識する
62 eliminate: 除く

and a professor evaluating student work.

> **Check your understanding 2.4**
> Why are members of an in-group bias against members of an out-group?
> *Answer: In-groups are biased against out-groups in order to improve the self-esteem and confidence of the members of the in-group.*

Key points for Chapter 2

- ▶ A category is a collection of examples of similar objects, ideas, phenomena, and so on.
- ▶ People divide the world around them into categories.
- ▶ This categorization process is based on a combination of both cultural and inherent knowledge.
- ▶ A prototype is an abstract example of a category that consists of the common characteristics of the examples in the category.
- ▶ When you meet a person for the first time, you assign her to a category, assume that she is prototypical, and communicate with her accordingly[63].
- ▶ People tend to compare groups, and are biased towards groups to which they belong.
- ▶ People want their in-groups to be better than out-groups because it raises their self-esteem.

---

63 accordingly: それに応じて

Categories, Prototypes, and Groups

PRACTICE QUESTIONS

Q 2.1 Match the items on the left with the categories on the right on a one-to-one basis[64].

computer	VEHICLE
pink	FRUIT
bicycle	PET
hamster	TOOL
orange	CUSTOM
bowing	COLOR

Q 2.2 Write down examples of prototypical and non-prototypical members of the following categories. The first two have already been done for you.

Category	Prototypical Member	Non-Prototypical Member
SPORT	baseball	darts
お酒	日本酒	みりん
PET		
大学		
HOBBY		
FLAVOR OF CANDY		
女性の下の名前		

Q 2.3 List some characteristics of a prototypical member of the category ROBOT. How much intelligence does it have? What type of senses[65] does it have? What type of movements can it perform? Draw a

---

64 one-to-one basis: 一対一の組み合わせ
65 senses: sense の複数形；感覚，五感

cartoon drawing of a prototypical robot and a non-prototypical robot.

Q 2.4 Following is a list of some of the courses you can take at a university. Arrange the list in order from most prototypical to least prototypical.

心理学と詐欺
宇宙観光経済論
マンガの書き方
物理学入門
ロープワーク（ヒモやロープの縛り方）

Q 2.5 For each of the following categories, list two prototypical members and then decide if the category is based on cultural knowledge or inherent knowledge.

DANCE　　　　PAIN　　　　JUNK FOOD
JOKE　　　　EMOTION

Q 2.6 a. Following is a list of food items. Circle the items that are fruits. Stop after 10 seconds. Ready, set, go!

りんご　　　いちご　　　オリーブ
ココナツ　　梅　　　　　メロン
梨　　　　　レモン　　　ひょうたん
トマト　　　かぼちゃ　　すいか

b. Make a list of the characteristics of the category FRUIT. Try to think of at least four characteristics. Give one example of a food item that you circled in (a.) that has all of these characteristics.

Categories, Prototypes, and Groups

Q 2.7 The words 先輩 and 後輩 are two examples of categories. You change your language depending on which of these categories your addressee belongs to. For example, if your addressee belongs to the category 先輩, you use more polite language. What is the most important characteristic that separates these two groups?

    characteristic of the 先輩 category: _____

    characteristic of the 後輩 category: _____

Complete the following table using example members of the above two categories.

	prototypical example	non-prototypical example
Category: 先輩		
Category: 後輩		

Q 2.8 a. Make a list of four or five characteristics of a prototypical university student of 文学部. Do the same for a prototypical university student of 理工学部. If you belong to a 学部 that is quite different from these two, then make a list of a prototypical university student of your 学部.

  b. Now compare the lists you made in (a.). Which 学部 has more positive characteristics? Which one has more negative characteristics? Were you biased towards your in-group?

3 Audience Design and Communication Accommodation

This chapter introduces two important theories of communication: *Audience Design Theory* and *Communication Accommodation Theory*. The common theme of both is the speaker adjusting his speech to match the characteristics of the person he is talking to.

Audience design

In Chapter 1, I explained that your speech shows your own characteristics (page 11), and that you also adjust your speech to match the characteristics of the addressee (page 11). This chapter introduces another source of influence on the way you speak: the audience.

■ The audience
The **audience** refers[1] not only to the people the speaker is talking to, but also to everyone who can hear the speaker. Consider the following example. You are standing in line with a friend, waiting to buy tickets for a movie. You are talking to your friend in a loud voice about your favorite actor.

---

1 refer: 言及する

Your friend is naturally a part of the audience. Besides your friend, there are other people who can hear you, such as the person standing in line behind you. Now imagine that this person behind you is talking on her cell phone. Your voice is loud enough to be transmitted[2] through the cell phone to the person on the other end. Therefore, this person can also hear you, and is also part of your audience, even though you most likely do not realize it. Thus, the audience is made up of the following types of people:

- **addressee**（聞き手）
- **overhearer**（偶然聞く人）
- **eavesdropper**（盗み聞く人）

The *Audience Design Theory* (Bell 1984) states[3] that you design your speech not only for the addressee, but for the entire audience. Furthermore, the theory claims[4] that the order of influence on your speech is as follows:

1. speaker
2. addressee
3. overhearer
4. eavesdropper

You, as the speaker, naturally have the most influence over your speech. For example, if you are female, you will speak in a feminine way. If you are from Osaka, you will use the Osaka dialect[5].

The next largest influence on your speech is the addressee. For example, if you are from Osaka but are talking to a person from Tokyo, you tend to use less Osaka dialect.

After the addressee are the overhearers. You are not talking directly to these people, but you know they are there, and you thus adjust your speech.

---

2 transmit: 送信する
3 state: 述べる
4 claim: 主張する
5 dialect: 方言

Imagine that you are a university student from Osaka talking to a classmate from Tokyo. Most of the other students in the classroom are from Kansai. You will most likely tend to use the Kansai dialect. Now imagine that most of the other students in the classroom are from Kanto. You will tend to use less Kansai dialect now. Hence[6], you are adjusting your speech to match whether the overhearers are from Kansai or are from Kanto.

The last group is the eavesdroppers. Although they can hear you, you cannot see them. You do not know that they are listening, and you do not know who they are, so they have the smallest influence on your speech.

■ An example from a ski resort

A young male skier has just arrived at a ski resort. He boards[7] the ski lift, which carries people to the top of the mountain. He is sitting beside another young male skier whom he does not know. They have the following conversation about the snow conditions.

Skier #1 :	How's the snow, man?
Skier #2 :	It's fucking great, dude[8].
Skier #1 :	I heard it was shitty today.
Skier #2 :	That's bullshit[9], man[10].

The skiers are both young males, and they are using profanity[11], language that is typical[12] of young males. They are up high on a ski lift, and so they

---

6 hence: そのゆえに，したがって
7 board: 搭乗する
8 dude: 奴，お前；this word is often used as a 感動詞 between young males
9 bullshit: 雄牛の糞；in this context it means「嘘だろう！」
10 In this context, this word is the same as "dude"
11 profanity: 罵り言葉
12 typical of A: A らしい

need not worry about what others will think of their rude language. In this situation, the language being used is influenced by only the speaker characteristics (young male) and the addressee characteristics (also young male).

Now consider a slightly different scenario. This time, the two skiers are standing in line waiting to board the ski lift. They now have the same conversation. However, now there are other people also waiting in line. In other words, now there are overhearers around them. Furthermore, some of these overhearers are children. These two young men do not normally use profanity in front of children. This time their conversation goes like this:

Skier #1 :	How's the snow, man?
Skier #2 :	It's really great, dude.
Skier #1 :	I heard it was sucky[13] today.
Skier #2 :	That's crap[14], man.

Compare the second conversation with the first. Both conversations use slang words found in the speech of young males. However the first conversation uses profanity whereas the second conversation does not. The audience, which contains[15] young children, is influencing the speech of the young men. Note that the characteristics of the speaker and the addressee are still more important than the characteristics of the overhearers; the speakers still talk like men.

> *Check your understanding 3.1*
>
> Imagine that you are watching a movie scene, and one actor is talking to another one. Identify the speaker, addressee, overhearer, and eavesdropper.

---

13 sucky: 最悪 ; often used as verb, as in "That sucks!"
14 crap: 糞 ; in this context it means「嘘だろう!」; "crap" is much politer than "shit"
15 contain: 含める

> *Answer:* The speaker and the addressee are the two actors. The overhearers are people who are listening to them, and those whom the actors are aware of, such as the camera crew and the director. The eavesdroppers are people who are listening to the actors that the actors are not aware of, such as the viewers of the movie. According to the theory, all of these people, including you as the viewer, influence the speech of the actor who is talking.

■ An example from my own experience

I often experience the effect of the overhearer influencing the speech of the speaker in my daily life in Japan. I am a very tall Caucasian, and I am obviously not Japanese. Because I am tall, I stand out in a crowd, and people easily notice me. My presence[16] seems to sometimes influence the speech of Japanese people around me, even though they are strangers and they are not talking to me. Let me give you an example.

A Japanese man and his two daughters were waiting at a traffic light to cross the street. I walked up and stood beside them. I was also waiting to cross the street. It was a cold day, and one of the daughters was not wearing a coat. She looked like she was becoming cold.

> father: おまえ、どうしてコート着てない？
> daughter: だってさ、かあさんがいらんやろうって
> father: おまえ、ばかや！
> daughter: かあさんがばか！
> *Father turned to the younger daughter.*
> father: お姉ちゃんは頭がパー
> *They laugh; father turns back to the older daughter.*

16　presence: 存在

| father: | Fool, fool, you fool[17]. |
| daughter: | かあさんがばかって！ |

The older daughter was between twelve and fourteen years old. They were obviously Japanese, and spoke Japanese to each other. So why did the father suddenly switch to English in the middle of the conversation? Of course, we cannot know for sure, but most likely I influenced the speech of the father. I obviously look like an English speaker, so my presence influenced the father to speak English, even though he was not talking directly to me.

Communication accommodation

The previous section explained how the audience influences the speech of the speaker. In this section, we look at how the speech of the addressee influences the speech of the speaker. This type of influence has been researched in detail, and a social psychological theory called *Communication Accommodation*[18] *Theory* (Giles & Smith 1979) has been developed. This section introduces two important ideas of the theory: convergence and divergence. I will give definitions of these ideas shortly. Before I do that, let me begin with an example.

In 1984, a researcher published a report about the speech of a travel agent[19] (Coupland 1984). The researcher recorded the speech of a woman for one entire day while she was working as a travel agent. As a travel agent, an important part of her job was talking to customers on the

---

17 Grammatically, this English is mistaken. It should be "you are a fool".
18 accommodation: 収容；this word also means 宿泊施設
19 travel agent: 旅行代理業者

telephone, and she was recorded talking on the telephone many times throughout the day. A careful study of her speech revealed[20] an interesting fact: She changed her speech style every time she spoke on the telephone. Sometimes she used standard accent, while other times she used dialect.

The researcher focused on her pronunciation of the sound /t/ in order to study this phenomenon. The sound /t/ has different pronunciations in different dialects of English, particularly when it is in the middle of a word. Table 3.1 lists three different ways that /t/ is pronounced. The linguistics symbol and name are also given for each sound. The first variant[21] is from American English, and sounds like a "d." In American English, the words *writer* and *rider* sound the same. Other examples of words that sound the same are *ladder/latter*, and *catty/caddy*.

Dialect	Symbol	Linguistics Name	Description
American English	ɾ	alveolar flap	sounds like a "d"; the words *writer* and *rider* sound the same
Standard British English	t	alveolar stop	a "t" sound, similar to the sound of a /t/ at the beginning of words
British English dialects, such as Cockney dialect	ʔ	glottal stop	the sudden stopping and starting of sound; written in Japanese as ッ, as in the expression あッ; in British English dialect, the word *water* is pronounced as ワッアー

Table 3.1: Different pronunications of the sound /t/ in English

The second variant is from Standard British English, and sounds like the "t" at the beginning of words, such as the /t/ sound in the word *tip*. The

---

20 reveal: 明らかにする

21 variant: 変異形；different forms of the same sound, word, etc. For example, variants of the word「です」are「だ」,「でございます」,「や」, and「じゃ」.

third variant is from British dialects such as Cockney English, the dialect spoken around London, England. The "t" sound is a break in the flow of sound. This sound is represented in Japanese by ッ, as in the expression 「あッ」. For example, the word *water* is pronounced as 「ワッアー」 in Cockney English[22].

As for the travel agent, she used both the Standard British variant and the British dialect variant. Furthermore, she mixed the two variants, for example, using one variant in one sentence and then using the other variant in the next sentence. Examining her pronunciation of /t/ in each phone call showed that the number of times a variant was used changed from phone call to phone call, as shown in Figure 3.1. This figure shows the percentage use of the British dialect variant of /t/ by the travel agent and the customer in four of the recorded calls.

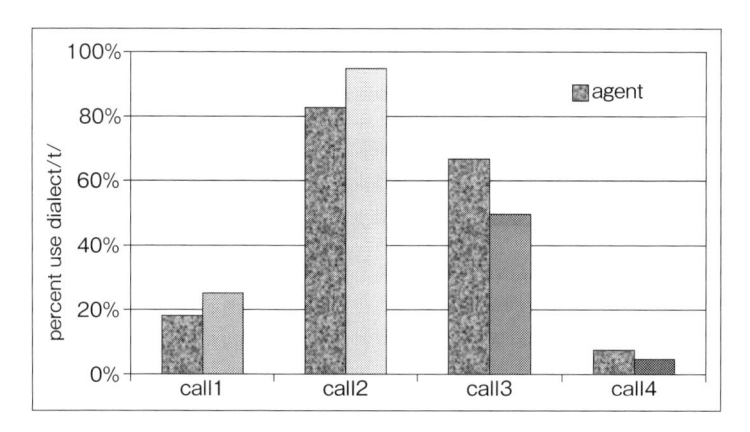

Figure 3.1: The percentage use of the dialect variant of /t/ by a travel agent and the customers she was talking to

---

22 This third variant also occurs in American English before sounds such as "n," so that, for example, in both Cockney English and American English, the word *eaten* is pronounced 「イイッン」.

As the figure shows, the travel agent's usage[23] of the pronunciation variants for /t/ was not random. The researcher also recorded the speech of the customers, and then compared the pronunciation of /t/ by the travel agent with the pronunciation of /t/ by the customers. This comparison showed that in every case, the travel agent adjusted her usage of the dialect variant of /t/ so that it closely resembled[24] the patterns of variation usage of the customer. If the customer tended[25] to use a lot of the dialect sounds, then the travel agent also tended to us a lot of the dialect sounds, as in the case of call 4. Similarly, if the customer frequently tended to use the standard pronunciation variant, then the travel agent also used it frequently, as in the case of call 2.

This result is one example of several studies (see Giles & Ogay 2007) that leads to the following important conclusion:

> Speakers adjust their speech to make it sound more like the speech of the addressee

This adjustment is called **convergence**[26], and we say that the speaker converges with the addressee by making his or her speech more similar to the speech of the addressee.

Convergence of speech takes place all around us. For example, imagine that you are participating in a university student exchange program in order to study English at a foreign university. While at the foreign university, you meet other Japanese exchange students from different parts of Japan. You become friends and chat with each other in vernacular[27] Japanese. In Japan, the students normally use the local dialect of where

---

23　usage: (a linguistics word) 語法；言葉の文法や発音などの一例または全例
24　resemble: 似る
25　tend to use a lot: よく使う傾向がある
26　convergence: 一点への集合・集中，意見などの合致

they are from. However, these students cannot accommodate to each other by using local dialects, which are all different. Instead, they use mostly 共通語. The result is that the students tend to sound similar to each other.

Another example of convergence is talking to the opposite gender[28]. When a group of men talk together, they tend to talk in a very masculine way, using words like 「俺」, 「手前」, 「しやがる」, and 「ぬかす」. When one of these men then talks to a female friend, he adjusts his speech so that it is more feminine by using words such as 「僕」 and nicknames[29]. Similarly, women tend to adjust their speech so that it is more masculine when they talk to men.

Convergence tends to be mutual[30]. The speaker gradually adjusts his or her speech to sound more like the speech of the addressee. However, a conversation normally involves the participants taking turns talking. When it is the addressee's turn to talk, he becomes the speaker, and then adjusts his speech to sound more like the addressee. In this way, both the participants of a conversation are adjusting their speech towards some middle ground.

Research on communication accommodation has shown that we converge more than just with speech. Following are other examples of what we accommodate (Giles & Ogay 2007):

- how fast we talk
- how long we pause between sentences
- how loud we talk
- how big our hand gestures are when we talk
- how polite we are

---

27 vernacular: 日常口語の
28 opposite gender: 異性
29 nickname: あだ名
30 mutual: 互いの

This convergence process seems to influence our speech in many ways, and seems to work at the subconscious level. It is a very powerful process, and it is important to our communication.

> **Check your understanding 3.2**
> You are chatting with your friend. Your friend becomes excited and begins to talk quickly. According to *Communication Accommodation Theory*, how will you adjust your speech?
> *Answer: According to the theory, you will adjust your speech to make it more like your friend's speech. That is, you will also speak faster.*

■ Why do we converge?

Why do we converge our speech? Recall that convergence makes your speech more like the speech of the addressee. Researchers have concluded that this process reduces social distance[31], and creates a feeling of closeness (Giles & Ogay 2007). This idea fits nicely with the idea of the group, which was introduced in Chapter 2 (page 27). You naturally feel close to other people in your in-groups. Therefore, you talk to other people in your in-group in a way that reduces social distance. Because converging your speech with the speech of the addressee reduces social distance, this is one way you can reduce social distance when talking to another member of an in-group. The close social distance created by accommodation in turn reinforces[32] in-group membership.

Closer social distance has other advantages too, other than reinforcing group membership. For example, people tend to believe and trust other

---

31 social distance: 社会的な距離. In English, we talk about relationships with words about distance, such as a <u>close</u> relationship (親近感), or to feel <u>distant</u> from someone (疎外感), as in the example sentence, *I am not so close to my father, but I am very close to my mother*.
32 reinforce: 強化する，補強する

people that they feel close to. You would naturally tell a secret to a friend, but would probably not tell your boss the same secret, because you trust your friend more than you trust your boss. Also, if you need help or sympathy[33], it is easier to get it from a person that you feel socially close to. I will return to these points when I present a more detailed discussion of communication accommodation by salespeople.

We adjust our speech to sound more like other members of our in-groups in order to reduce social distance. What about people who are not members of our in-group? There are often times when reducing social distance would be awkward[34] or socially unacceptable. For example, normally it is socially unacceptable for students to talk to professors the same way they talk to their close friends. In contrast, there are other times when you actually want to increase social distance. I give one example below. As I said, accommodation reduces social distance. How, then, do we increase social distance? The answer is to do the opposite: make our speech less like the speech of the person we are talking to. This is called **divergence**[35].

Divergence is used to maintain social distance between a speaker and an addressee (Giles & Ogay 2007). Returning to the example of the student talking to the professor, even if the professor uses ため口 towards the student, the student may still use 敬語 towards the professor. By not talking the same way, the student maintains social distance with that professor. Social distance is maintained because doing so is considered polite.

Another reason to diverge is to establish out-group membership. Consider the situation when students from the Kansai area meet students from the Kanto area for the first time. If the students from Kansai continue to speak in only the Kansai dialect, even while among students from Kanto,

---

33   sympathy: 同情
34   awkward: 不器用な
35   divergence: 一点から分かれ出ること，分岐，意見などの相違

then the Kansai students are creating social distance and establishing that the Kanto students are not members of the same group.

Another time that people diverge their speech from that of the addressee is when they disagree. Finally, recall that convergence reduces social distance, something that is done to show trust. The opposite, divergence, indicates[36] that you do not believe or trust the addressee. Here is an example of divergence during an argument that was posted[37] on an internet bulletin board titled お悩み掲示板[38]:

> バツイチで年上の嫁の話しです。
> 日常生活をしていると、些細な事で揉めたりしますよね？
> その場合、話し合いで解決したいと思っているのですが、うちの嫁は話し合うのが嫌いなのか、俺と話したくないのか都合が悪くなる度に、敬語になります。
> 子供も、そんな母の態度に？？？って感じで、雰囲気が悪くなります。
> 最近では、敬語に切り替わった時は、俺も敬語に切り替えます。
> ［省略］
> 嫁の気持ちが理解できる方がいたら、厳しいレスでもいいのでお願いします m(_ _)m
> 子供達は可愛いし、ずっと一緒にいたいのですが、話し合いも出来ないし、理解できないので、この先何年も一緒に暮らす自信がありません。

The poster[39] describes how his wife uses 敬語 when they argue. Normally, a husband and wife will use タメ口 when they talk to each other, and so by switching to 敬語, the wife is diverging from the speech of the husband. The wife is using divergence to create social distance and reinforce the message

---

36 indicate: 指し示す
37 post: 掲示板に投稿する
38 お悩み掲示板：http://onayamifree.com/threadres/764277/
39 poster: a person who posts a message

that she disagrees with him.

> Check your understanding 3.3
> What is convergence? Why do we do it?
> *Answer: Converging is adjusting your speech to make it more like the speech of the person you are talking to. We do it in order to reduce social distance, and create feelings of closeness.*
> What is divergence? Why do we do it?
> *Answer: Divergence is adjusting your speech to make it less like the speech of the person you are talking to. We do it in order to increase social distance, to show that we do not trust the other person, or to show disagreement.*

■ A detailed example: Convergence by salespeople[40]

I began the discussion of communication accommodation by presenting the example of a travel agent converging with the speech of the customers while she was talking with them on the telephone. Salespeople often receive special training, during which they learn to converge their speech patterns with those of the customer. Here is a summary from a training manual (東照二 2009：114):

> Simply, use the same words they do, match their speech speed and mirror their gestures.
> (簡単にいうと、客が使っているのと同じ言葉を使い、客の話すスピードに合わせ、客のジェスチャーに合わせる。)

Why is convergence so important to salespeople? Recall that convergence reduces social distance, and that if you feel close to someone, you are more

---

40　This section is based on pages 114 to 116 of 東照二 (2009).

likely to trust them. In other words, by converging his speech, the salesperson becomes more believable, and is then more likely to successfully sell something.

Salespeople learn not only to converge to the speech patterns of the customer, but also to match the sales pitch[41] to the lifestyle of the customer. For example, salespeople are trained to classify customers into categories based on prototypes. In Chapter 2, categories (page 18) and prototypes (page 26) were discussed. Table 3.2 lists four examples of categories and gives prototypical speech patterns for each category.

After identifying the category the customer belongs to, the salesperson then uses words that suit the lifestyle of a prototypical member of that category. Table 3.2 also lists examples of vocabulary that a salesperson might use with each of the categories of customers. For example, a salesperson is trying to sell a new car to a customer. The salesman decides that this customer fits the category of "patient, plodder". The salesperson then describes a new car as follows:

This model has been on the market for eight years, and has proven to be both durable[42] and reliable[43]. Its safety record is outstanding. It will make an excellent family vehicle. Let's take a look inside so you can see how comfortable it is.

---

41 sales pitch: 売り込みのための交渉, 売り込み口上
42 durable: 長持ちする
43 reliable: 信頼できる

Category	Prototypical speech pattern	Example Vocabulary
doer, driver （実行型）	quickly gets to the point; when excited speaks faster	results performance fast save time now efficient your opinion you
persuader, socializer （説得型、社交型）	uses many adjectives, and tends to exaggerate; often uses gestures	latest stylish trendy status fashion colourful exciting contemporary popular
patient, plodder （忍耐型、ボソボソ型）	speaks slowly and gently; often expresses emotions and feelings	durable traditional sturdy family lasting safe comfortable secure
analytical, controller （分析型、管理型）	speaks slowly and carefully selects words to say; talks after some thought	facts functional guaranteed precise state-of-the-art improved exact thorough

Table 3.2: Categories of customers, their prototypical speeh patterns, and example vocabulary used by a salesperson with customers from that category (adopted from pages 114 to 115 of 東照二 (2009))

This description uses the words that match the lifestyle of a prototypical member of the PLODDER category. By talking in this way, the salesperson converges with the customer's speech patterns, and thus reduces social distance. The reduction of social distance makes the salesperson sound more believable. All of this leads to a much greater chance of selling a car to the customer, and so converging with the customer is a very important when you are selling something. The next time you are trying to sound appealing[44], perhaps selling something at your part-time job, or perhaps trying to make a good impression with an attractive member of the opposite sex, focus on converging your speech style and vocabulary with your addressee. If you do so skillfully, then the person you are talking to should have a positive image of you.

---

44 appealing: 魅力的な

Key points for Chapter 3

▶ A speaker adjusts his speech to suit not only the addressee, but also other people who can hear the speaker talk.

▶ The order of influence on the speech of the speaker is:
1. speaker
2. addressee
3. overhearer
4. eavesdropper

▶ A speaker accommodates an addressee by making his speech sound more like the speech of the addressee. This phenomenon is called convergence.

▶ Convergence reduces social distance, which makes the speaker sound friendly and more believable.

▶ In some situations, a speaker will make her speech sound more different than the speech of the addressee. This phenomenon is called divergence.

▶ Divergence is used to increase social distance and to signal that the speaker disagrees with the addressee.

PRACTICE QUESTIONS

Q 3.1 a. Two young girls from a junior high school in Osaka went on a field trip to Kamakura. While there, they spoke Standard Japanese to the local hotel staff and the store clerks[45]. Is this convergence or divergence? Explain your decision.

b. While the two girls were sightseeing, they less often used the Osaka dialect than when at home. Why might that be? Hint: Who are the overhearers?

Q 3.2 The *Audience Design Model* claims that the addressee has more influence on the speaker's speech than the overhearer. Why might this be? Explain in your own words why you think that the addressee has more influence on the speaker's speech than the overhearer.

Q 3.3 A quiz show[46] is a popular type of television show in which a **host**[47] asks **participants** trivia[48] questions while an **audience** watches in the background. Besides these people, there is one more important group of people: the **viewers** watching the television show in their homes. Classify each of these groups of people as either *speaker*, *addressee*, *overhearer*, or *eavesdropper*, and then rank[49] these four groups of people in order of the amount of influence they have on the host's speech.

---

45 store clerk: 店員
46 quiz show: クイズ番組
47 host: 司会者
48 trivia: 豆知識
49 rank: 順位をつける

Q 3.4 Following are two translations of *Anne of Green Gables*「赤毛のアン」[50]. The translations are of the SAME words, yet the translations are very different. The translations are written by different translators, but this is not enough to explain the differences. Use the *Audience Design Model* to explain why the translations are so different. Hint: These are books, and so now the audience is expanded to also include the readers. What type of people do you think might read each of these translations?

> 翻訳 A:
> わがいとしのダイアナへ
> もちろん、あなたがお母さんの言いつけに従わなくてはならないからといって、わたしわるくなんか思わないわ。わたしたちの心は結ばれているんですもの。あなたの美しい贈り物は永久に大切にいたします。
> ……
> 今夜あなたのお手紙を枕の下にして眠るつもりです。
>
> 翻訳 B:
> あたしのダイアナ
> もちろん、あたし、あなたのことを怒ってなんかいません。だって、お母さんの言うことは聞かなければいけないにきまっているんですから。あたしたち、別れていても、心はいつも一つにつながっているのよね。あなたからのすてきなプレゼント、いつまでも大切にします。
> ……
> あなたの手紙、あたし、今夜、枕の下に入れて寝るつもりよ。

Q 3.5 Create one example of convergence and one example of divergence based on events in your daily life. For each example:

---

50 The Japanese translations are from pages 112 and 113 of 東照二 (2009).

Audience Design and Communication Accommodation

- describe who you are talking to
- describe how you adjust your speech
- explain why you adjust your speech that way

Q 3.6 Go back and reread the example post from the internet bulletin board お悩み掲示板 (page 52). The post illustrates an example of divergence. Explain in your own words what it is and why it is divergence. Carefully reread the post one more time. The post also gives an example of convergence. What is it? Explain in your own words what it is and why it is convergence.

Q 3.7 Explain why salespeople accommodate. Begin by explaining the effect of accommodation on social distance. Then explain the relationship between social distance and being able to sell something.

Q 3.8 Table 3.2 lists four types of customers. What type do you fit the closest? Write a sales pitch designed to sell your type of person a new car. Make use of the prototypical speech patterns and example vocabulary in Table 3.2 as you write your sales pitch.

4 Culture and Miscommunication

This section introduces several topics in intercultural communication. This chapter begins with a definition what culture is, and concludes with an explanation on the reasons for cultural miscommunication[1]. Chapters 5 and 6 then introduce several areas of communication that differ with culture, such as nonverbal communication, ways of apologizing, and emphasis[2] of a culture: the group or the individual.

What is culture?

To understand intercultural communication, we first need to understand what culture is. When asked for examples of Japanese culture, most students talk about concrete[3], visible objects or actions such as samurai and eating sushi. However, anthropologists[4] would agree that the action of eating sushi is not culture. Sushi is often eaten in Canada, and yet eating sushi is not normally considered to be a part of Canadian culture. Instead,

---

1 miscommunication: コミュニケーション上の誤解
2 emphasis: 強調されたもの
3 concrete: 具体的な
4 anthropologist: 人類学者

definitions of culture refer to more abstract[5] ideas (for example, Danesi 2008):

> Culture is the set of shared attitudes, values, goals, and practices that characterizes a group.

Thus, the action of eating sushi is not to be considered a part of Japanese culture; rather Japanese culture includes the custom of eating raw fish, and the attitudes and opinions about raw fish that are shared by most Japanese people. In other words, Japanese culture is the collection of:

- knowledge
- values
- beliefs
- customs
- attitudes

In order for something (knowledge, values, and so on) to be considered as culture, it must be shared by most of the people of that culture. For example, most Japanese people have a positive attitude towards eating raw fish.

Let's take the example of cures for the common cold[6]. Japanese students often tell me that if I have a cold, I should not have a bath. In contrast, Westerners believe the opposite: if you catch a cold, you should heat up your body by having a hot bath, and by eating hot chicken noodle soup. These beliefs about cures for the common cold are examples of the differences between cultures.

Check your understanding 4.1
According to the definition presented here, which of these belongs to

---

5 abstract: 抽象的な
6 cure for the common cold: かぜの治療方法

> Japanese culture?
> a. 漫画 such as *One Piece* and *Doraemon*
> b. positive attitudes towards reading 漫画
> c. the belief that 招き猫 is good luck for business
> d. the custom of bowing
>
> Answer: b; c; d. The first one does not belong to Japanese culture because these 漫画 are not knowledge, values, beliefs, customs or attitudes. They are actual things.

■ Cultural stereotypes

People use their own culture (i.e., their beliefs, attitudes, knowledge) when they interact[7] with the world around them. In general, this is not a problem. However, if you interact with members of another culture, then basing[8] the interaction on your own culture creates problems. Part of your own culture is a collection of beliefs and attitudes about people from other cultures. Recall from Chapter 2 (page 26) that when you meet someone, you assign them to a category, and then assume that they have the prototypical characteristics of people of the category. For example, if you meet a Westerner, you naturally assume that they are a prototypical Westerner, and that they speak English fluently. This is in spite[9] of the fact that many Westerners do not speak English fluently.

These assumptions about people based on prototypical behavior are called **cultural stereotypes**. Cultural stereotypes are a source of friction[10] and miscommunication between people of different cultures (八代京子 et al.

---

7 interact: 相互に影響する，交流する
8 basing A on B: A を B に基づける
9 in spite of the fact that: ということにもかかわらず
10 friction: 摩擦

2001: 16). For example, many Westerners believe that Japanese people are very hard-working. Of course, this is not always true. There are many hard-working Japanese people (including you, right?) but there are also many Japanese people who would be considered lazy, or perhaps work hard at something other than studying or working, such as playing video games. This stereotype about Japanese people leads to scenarios such as the following.

> A Canadian landlord[11] is looking for a tenant[12] for an empty apartment. He is worried about the noise levels because he has had some complaints[13] in the past. He interviews candidates[14] including a Japanese exchange student. He decides to rent the apartment to the Japanese exchange student, believing that the student will be studying hard all of the time, and therefore will be quiet. However, the Japanese exchange student does not study much. Furthermore, his hobby is playing base guitar, and he turns out to be a very noisy tenant. This leads to problems and friction between the tenant and the landlord.

These problems could have been avoided if the landlord realized that he was basing his decision on a cultural stereotype, and that people are all different.

Surface culture and hidden culture

When you live in a culture different from the one that you grew up in, you

---

11 landlord: 家主
12 tenant: 入居者
13 complaint: 愚痴, 文句
14 candidate: 候補者

begin to learn about that culture. Some aspects[15] of a culture can be learned very quickly. For example, non-Japanese who begin living in Japan quickly learn customs such as removing your shoes at the entrance of a house, and having a bath in the evening[16]. However, other aspects of a culture are much more difficult to learn. Consider the following scenario. You are talking with your friend and suddenly your cell phone rings. You want to answer the call. What is considered the polite thing to do here?

When Japanese people interrupt[17] a conversation with their friend in order to answer a call, the normal, socially-expected behavior is to give a short apology, such as「ごめんね」, or「ちょっとすみません」, or even to say nothing at all. There is certainly no explanation given of who called. However, Western culture is very different. First, an apology would be considered awkward[18] among friends. Instead, a phrase such as "just one second[19]" is considered appropriate. More importantly, in Western culture, some sort of an explanation of the call is expected. This is normally a brief description of who called and why they called. Here is an example: "That was my cousin. She called to cancel our lunch date." So you can see from this example that the appropriate behavior when interrupting a conversation with a friend is very different in Japan and in the West. The next chapter includes several more similar examples, such as those on cultural expectations about apologizing and giving compliments[20].

Unlike, for example, removing your shoes when you enter a house,

---

15　aspect: 物事の一つの面，様相
16　The Western custom is to have a shower in the morning. Having a bath is not common.
17　interrupt: 妨げる，さえぎる
18　awkward: 不器用な
19　just one second: literally, ただの一秒 ; it means "Please wait for a very short amount of time."
20　compliment: 褒め言葉

cultural customs and expectations about interrupting a conversation to answer the call are more difficult to learn. These two types of culture (easy and difficult to learn) are given different names. Culture that is easy to learn is called **surface culture**. Culture that is difficult to learn is called **hidden culture**. Hidden culture is difficult to learn because, as the name suggests, the clues to that aspect of culture are usually hidden from view (八代京子 et al. 2001: 26). Of course, the clues to hidden culture are observable during the very brief time in which they appear, but at other times, they remain hidden. For example, consider the Western custom about giving an explanation after answering a call. Other than the actual explanation, there are no visible clues that such a custom even exists[21]: it is hidden. In contrast, consider the Japanese custom of taking shoes off at the entrance of a house. This custom produces a visible result: shoes are left at the entrance. Because you can see the result, such culture is called surface culture, and it is easier to learn than hidden culture.

When people who have had little or no exposure[22] to another culture think about that culture, they tend to think about surface culture. This is because surface culture is easier to observe and therefore it is easier to remember. For the same reason, when people live abroad, they quickly learn about the surface culture. However, aspects of the hidden culture take longer to learn. Thus, hidden culture is often a source of cultural miscommunication. This is illustrated by the following story posted on the internet[23] by a non-Japanese person. The website is titled *Japanese culture: A Primer*[24] *for Newcomers*.

---

21 exist: 存在する
22 exposure: 晒すこと，触れさせること；be exposed to another culture: 異文化に触れる
23 Japanese Culture: A Primer for Newcomers: http://www.thejapanfaq.com/FAQ-Primer.html
24 primer: 入門

> ### "Let's have dinner together sometime." -- A Culture Clash
>
> In the West when someone says to another "let's have dinner together sometime", it usually means "let's have dinner together sometime". Sounds like an invitation, doesn't it? And if you're new in town, don't have a lot of friends yet, and are looking for a date, it sounds even better. Unfortunately, if a Japanese person says that or "come over to my place sometime" to you, what he/she really might mean is "I hope we get along well together." Is this more than a little confusing? I had two big shocks from this myself. When I first started working at a company, a secretary (the cute one everybody wanted to date) told me this. Now, if the other five or six secretaries all said the same thing to me as a matter of etiquette[25], I would've caught on[26] immediately. But only one did, and after agreeing on a date and time, I got stood up[27]. I dismissed it as a misunderstanding[28], but when a similar situation occurred again later, I finally got the message. So let this be a warning -- take offers with a grain of salt[29]. Unless specific details like a date and time are mentioned, don't hold your breath[30]. If you're really interested, leave your phone number, tell the person to call you anytime, but don't sit waiting by the phone Saturday night.

The person who wrote this story is probably familiar with Japanese culture; he is working in Japan. Yet, he still received a huge shock after being invited out for dinner and then being stood up. The Japanese term for polite

---

25 etiquette: 礼儀, エチケット
26 to catch on: to understand; literally 掴む
27 to get stood up: 異性の人にふられる
28 dismiss: 解雇, 解散, 棄却; *dismiss as a misunderstanding* 誤解だと退ける
29 take with a grain of salt: 真剣に考えない, 話半分に聞く; literally 塩一粒と摂取する
30 don't hold your breath: あまり期待しない; *hold your breath* 息を止める (固唾を呑む)

phrases such as 「遊びに来て下さい」 and 「一緒に食べに行こう」 is 社交辞令. People who are familiar with Japanese culture know that these polite words have no substance[31], and such invitations are not meant to be followed up. In fact, there is even a Japanese word for the natural disappearance of such invitations: 自然消滅. The reason why the author of this internet post does not know the customs for 社交辞令 and 自然消滅 is because these are examples of hidden culture, and hidden culture is more difficult to learn about than surface culture.

I began this section by defining[32] culture as the collection of common knowledge, values, beliefs, customs and attitudes. While there are many aspects of culture that have visible clues, from this list it is easy to see that there are also many aspects that do not. For example, much common knowledge, such as the knowledge that asking an acquaintance[33] how old they are is considered to be rude in the West but not in Japan, does not have any visible clues. Because a large portion[34] of culture is hidden, cultural misunderstandings are common. However, now that you know about hidden culture, you can pay close attention to it and look for it. This is the first step to learning about hidden culture and avoiding cultural misunderstanding when you live abroad.

Check your understanding 4.2

Which of the following is surface culture and which is hidden culture?

a. the custom of exchanging greeting cards[35]

b. the custom of 根回し

---

31 substance: 本質, 内容
32 define: 定義する
33 acquaintance: 知人
34 portion: a part; 部分
35 greeting cards: 名刺

> c. the positive attitudes about 漫画
>
> d. the negative attitudes towards sun tanning[36], particularly among women
>
> *Answer: In order to answer this question, ask yourself, "How easy is it to see the results of these aspects of Japanese culture?" Items a., c. and d. all produce very visible[37] results and therefore are surface culture. In contrast, b. is hidden culture.*

Gender, culture, and miscommunication

One scenario in which miscommunication occurs even though the participants in the conversation have the same cultural background is communication between the members of the opposite sex[38]. In order to illustrate[39] this point, I present the following story[40]:

> This story is about a fourth year Japanese university student named Sae, who is quite busy looking for employment. In this university, students begin job hunting once they became fourth year students. At this time, her biggest concern, besides job hunting, is the future of her relationship with her boyfriend, Kenta. Kenta, who is a year younger than Sae, is a third year student and not yet concerned about graduation and job hunting. Furthermore, Sae cannot tell if Kenta takes their relationship seriously. At times, Kenta does not seem very enthusiastic, but at other times, he is quite passionate. Sae really wants Kenta to

---

36 sun tan: 日焼けする
37 visible: 目に見える，可視の
38 opposite sex: 異性
39 illustrate: 実例や図解を使って説明する
40 This is story is an abbreviated version of pages 73 to 75 of 久米 & 長谷川 (2007).

make clear his feelings towards her, but she worries that if she confronts[41] him, he will become angry at her. She could not decide what to do. Eventually summer arrived without Sae coming to any decision about her relationship with Kenta.

Then one day, Sae received a job offer[42] from a company in Tokyo. Sae thought to herself, "If I tell Kenta what will he do? Will he be angry? Or will he be happy for me?" She decided to be brave and tell Kenta on their next date, even though it had been awhile since she had last seen him. However, upon hearing the news, Kenta replied brusquely[43], "That's nice," and began to talk about a movie he saw on television recently.

Sae was shocked at Kenta's indifference towards what was not only an important decision for her but also for him as well. She became angry, "If you don't want me in your life, then fine! I just wish you had told me sooner." This was followed by a brief period of silence, and then Sae continued by listing the several things she had put up with[44]: "You only listen half-heartedly whenever I tell you about my problems. You just respond, 'sucks[45] to be you,' as if you are not interested in my life at all. When I was really upset because my job hunting was not going well, you didn't want to listen, and instead said let's go to a movie. You are a pathetic excuse for a boyfriend![46]" Kenta was so surprised by what Sae said that he was simply dumbfounded[47].

41　confront: 立ち向かう，対決する
42　job offer: 内定
43　brusquely: 無愛想に，そっけなく
44　things she had put up with: 我慢してきた事
45　sucks (slang): 最悪
46　You are a pathetic excuse for a boyfriend: あなたは最低の彼氏だ
47　dumbfounded: 唖然とする

The last line of the story suggests that Kenta was not intentionally[48] trying to make Sae angry. He was completely surprised by her sudden anger. This conflict came from a misunderstanding between Sae and Kenta. To understand how such misunderstandings are possible, let's first look at the differences between how young boys and girls play, and then we'll discuss gender-specific communication styles.

■ Gender-specific play styles of children

Researchers believe that misunderstanding between men and women is a type of cultural misunderstanding. Gender communication researchers[49] propose the theory that men and women have their own culture within the larger culture of a society. Researchers studying communication among children have made the following observations (Wood & Reich 2006: 179-180):

- boys and girls tend to play only with other children of the same sex
- a typical group of boys and a typical group of girls have completely different play styles

These different play styles are believed to reflect[50] the differences between the genders. When boys play, they tend to do the following more than girls:

- be involved in a physical activity such as running
- argue and disagree
- be aggressive[51] or imitate[52] violence such as 戦隊ヒーローごっこ
- compete and determine who the best is or who the winner is
- talk at the same time

---

48 intentionally: わざと
49 For example, there is a well-known book about miscommunication between men and women by Deborah Tannen (1990) titled *You Just Don't Understand*.
50 reflect: 反映する
51 aggressive: 攻撃的な
52 imitate: まねる

In contrast, when girls play, they tend to do the following more than boys:
- sit or stay in one area
- negotiate[53] and agree
- cooperate
- ask questions
- take turns while talking

The two play styles are very different. The boys prefer physical activity and playing rough, while the girls prefer non-physical activity and cooperating with each other. Of course, many boys also often adopt[54] the feminine style of play, and many girls often adopt the masculine style of play. However, when large numbers of children are observed, the differences in play styles are clear.

■ Gender-specific conversational styles of adults

Researchers claim that the different play styles we learn as children become the basis for our way of interacting with other people the rest of our lives (Wood & Reich 2006: 181). As adults, men and women use conversation for very different purposes. Men use conversation for two purposes. The first purpose is completing a task. The second purpose is to establish their self-sufficiency[55] and their ability to do things. Men often talk about how to do something or how well something was done. There is a stereotype about men being reluctant[56] to ask for directions. Asking for directions acknowledges one's dependency[57] on others and a lack of self-sufficiency.

---

53 negotiate: 交渉する
54 adopt: 採用する
55 self-sufficiency: 自給自足
56 reluctant: いやいやながら
57 dependency: 依存状態

Women, on the other hand, use conversation to build intimacy[58] with other people (Wood & Inman 1993). Therefore, women enjoy sitting and talking with friends for long periods of time. In contrast, men build intimacy by doing something together, such as playing a sport. Men tend to be friends with the people they do things with, and accomplishing a task (such as scoring a goal in a soccer game) is often the central theme of the conversation (Wood & Inman 1993).

Also, male conversations have more of a tendency to show a social hierarchy[59] than female conversations, with some participants taking a leader role and others taking a follower role (Wood & Reich 2006). In female conversations, the participants tend to seek mutual[60] agreement. When a female participant takes a dominant leader role in a conversation, she risks that the other participants of the conversation will become angry.

These differences in conversational goals (building intimacy versus doing things) are reflected in the play styles of children. Boys' play is active and competitive. Likewise[61], men's conversations are about doing an activity and show social hierarchy. In contrast, girls' play involves negotiation and cooperation. Similarly, women's conversations also show negotiation and cooperation.

These differences in conversational styles between men and women lead to cultural miscommunication, the theme of this chapter. One example is the different responses when someone complains. Women see complaints as part of conversations. The act of complaining itself builds intimacy and so it alone is enough; often nothing else needs to be done other than listen to the complaint. Men, on the other hand, hear complaints as requests for a

---

58　intimacy: 親密感
59　social hierarchy: 社会階層
60　mutual: 相互の
61　likewise: 同じく，同様に

solution, and so either give advice or seek to resolve the problem. These different ways of viewing complaints leads to miscommunication when men and women complain to each other (久米 & 長谷川 2007: 76). For example, if a woman complains to a man, she may want nothing more than for him to listen to her and to agree with her. Instead of agreeing with her, he gives advice on what she should have done—advice she did not want. This results in misunderstanding, tension, and anger.

Now, go back now to the story of Sae and Kenta. That story illustrated these differences in communication styles. Kenta was not intentionally trying to make Sae angry; their communication styles were different and this was what made Sae angry. Sae wanted to build intimacy through words whereas Kenta wanted to use actions. For example, Sae wanted to talk about her job hunting and be comforted by Kenta when things were not going smoothly. On the other hand, Kenta wanted to go to a movie. This conflict could have easily been avoided. Kenta should have realized the importance of communication to Sae and made an effort to communicate. Even if he was not sure about the future, he should have at least said so.

> *Check your understanding 4.3*
> Which of the following groups of people has the most influence on the way we learn gender-related aspects of culture?
> a. our teachers
> b. our parents
> c. our friends of the opposite sex
> d. our friends of the same sex
>
> *Answer: d. We learn about gender-related aspects of culture as we grow up. During this period of our lives (from about 3 to 15 years of age), we spend most of our free time with friends of the same sex, and so they have the most influence on us.*

Key points for Chapter 4

▶ Culture is the set of shared attitudes, values, goals, and practices that characterizes a group.
▶ Stereotypes are assumptions about people based on cultural prototypes, and they are a source of miscommunication.
▶ There are two types of culture: surface culture and hidden culture. Surface culture is easy to learn. Hidden culture is difficult to learn.
▶ Hidden culture is often a source of miscommunication when people from different cultures communicate with each other.
▶ Young boys and girls have very different play styles. Researchers and theorists believe that these different play styles reflect differences between the genders.
▶ Men use conversation to accomplish a task or activity. They also use conversation to establish their self-sufficiency.
▶ Women use conversation to establish their membership in a group and to build intimacy with other group members.
▶ The gender-related differences between men and women sometimes cause cultural miscommunication when adults of the opposite sex talk to each other.

Culture and Miscommunication

PRACTICE QUESTIONS

Q 4.1 Do you think that primates[62] such as gorillas have culture? Use the definition of culture presented in this chapter (page 61). Explain why or why not?

Q 4.2 List five examples of Japanese surface culture and five examples of Japanese hidden culture.

Q 4.3 List five examples of Western surface culture and five examples of Western hidden culture. Did you have difficulty with the hidden culture items?

Q 4.4 a. Ask a friend or a family member who has never lived abroad to list ten things (either concrete or abstract) that they think are aspects of Western culture. How many are surface culture? How many are hidden culture? I had said that people who have little or no exposure to another culture tend to think more about surface culture. Do your results agree with this statement?

b. Now repeat the above exercise with someone who has live in a Western country for at least half a year. Did this person list more examples of hidden culture?

Q 4.5 The different communication styles of men and women were introduced in this chapter (page 68). Based on these differences, give an example of a speech action (either something said or a way

---

62 primate: 霊長類

of speaking) by a female university student talking to a group of female university students that would be considered divergence (page 51).

Q 4.6 a. Some people communicate exactly as per the gender-specific styles I described in this chapter (page 70), while others do not. Do you think that your male and female friends conform[63] to the gender-specific communication styles described in this chapter? Give examples of the ways in which your friends communicate to support your answer.

b. What about you? How well do these gender-specific communication styles match your own communication style? Give examples of the way in which you communicate to support your answer.

Q 4.7 Gender miscommunication is a problem in the workplace. Here is one case. A female manager was trying to explain her ideas about a project to a male manager. Although the male manager was listening, he did not say anything, did not nod[64] his head, and did not smile. About halfway through the explanation, the female manager said to the male manager that he was obviously not interested in what she had to say. She suddenly got up and left the room. However, the male manager was interested, and was very confused by her sudden anger. Explain why there is miscommunication between the male and female managers. What should the managers do to improve communication? Use the following ideas in your

---

63　conform: 一致する
64　nod: うなずく

answer: intercultural communication; gender-specific communication styles (page 70); hidden culture (page 65); bias against the out-group (page 28, assume that male and female managers are different groups); convergence (page 48) as a tool to reduce social distance.

5 Examples of Cultural Differences in Communication

This chapter gives several concrete examples of cultural differences in communication. The topics covered are disagreeing, apologizing, complimenting, maintaining eye contact, and touching. All of these are examples of hidden culture, which are difficult to learn and can easily lead to miscommunication.

Disagreement

When people are exposed[1] to a new culture, they are often surprised to discover that the reasons for disagreement and the ways of disagreement differ according to the culture. Consider the following story[2] about intercultural communication and differences in disagreement:

> This story is about Takahashi-san, a Japanese manager working in an American-affiliated company[3] in Tokyo. The company president, as well as several of the other managers, is American. The president and

---

1. exposed: expose の受身形 ; expose: 晒す
2. This story is based on page 43 of 八代 et al. (2001).
3. American-affiliated company: 日米の合併企業

the managers have weekly meetings in English. These meetings are not easy for Takahashi-san, as he is not fluent in English, and the non-Japanese tend to use a lot of colloquial[4] expressions when they chat among themselves. Takahashi-san has only spent a little time living abroad, and so he is barely able to keep up with[5] the conversation. However, he is a hard worker, and he is determined to perform well at the meetings.

While the first year of the company was not without problems, things were going smoothly, and Takahashi-san was quite proud of his role in the company. Then one day, Takahashi-san received a big shock. It turns out that his work performance was evaluated as not adequate[6].

It began with the usual weekly meeting of the managers and the company president. The main purpose of the meeting was for the company president to propose[7] a new idea to the managers and get feedback[8] on it. The American employees asked many questions about the idea, and soon everyone started debating[9] about the advantages and disadvantages of the idea. Takahashi-san also asked some questions, but in general, he thought that the ideas were good, and so he showed his support by staying quiet while others were criticizing[10] the idea. At the end of the meeting, the company president thanked everyone, and promised to revise[11] the original idea based on the discussion.

---

4 colloquial: 口語的な
5 keep up with: 付いて行く
6 adequate: 十分な，足りる
7 propose: 提案する
8 feedback: suggestions, comments, and criticisms about an idea; 提案，批判
9 debate: 討論する
10 criticize: 非難する
11 revise: 修正する，改良する

> After the meeting was over, the president called Takahashi-san into his office. He asked Takahashi-san why he did not participate in the meeting, and he seemed disappointed with Takahashi-san's contributions[12] to the weekly meetings in general. Takahashi-san was shocked. He felt that he always contributed to the meetings, and he could not understand why the company president was criticizing him. Takahashi-san promised that he would improve his performance, even though he had no idea what he had done wrong or how to improve.

Why was the American boss disappointed? What did Takahashi-san do wrong? It is not that Takahashi-san did anything wrong, but rather that he does not understand the differences between American and Japanese cultures with regards to arguments. These differences in culture lead to the cultural miscommunication and the boss's disappointment with Takahashi-san. Takahashi-san wanted to participate in the discussion, and he thought that he was participating by not disagreeing. However, the boss thought that he did not contribute to the discussion. This misunderstanding is an example of cultural miscommunication. The source of the miscommunication is the difference between the two (American and Japanese) cultures with regards to how and why disagreements occur.

The style of communication that the president was expecting Takahashi-san to use is called **debate style**. This style emphasizes[13] the following:
- explaining your opinions, actions, or decisions clearly
- asking questions about others' ideas or opinions
- disagreeing with others
- building up an idea through argument
- changing the original idea in response to criticism

---

12 contribution: 貢献，助力 ; in this story, the meaning is 発言
13 emphasize: 強調する

In this style of communication, participants[14] discuss an idea by arguing about it. The goal is to improve the idea. Participants intentionally[15] look for ways to criticize the idea and then openly do so. If someone thinks that it is a good idea then he argues against the criticism and defends the original idea. If the group feels that the criticism is good, then they will agree that there is a real problem with the original idea. A solution is sought[16] for the problem, and the original idea is modified[17] to include the agreed-upon solution. The process of criticizing is then repeated, and the original idea gradually changes as new problems and new solutions are found. The final result is believed to be an idea that is much better than the original idea.

This style of communication evolved[18] during over 2500 years of history of debating in the West (Russell 1946/2004). This history can be traced back[19] to ancient Greek civilization, and a place called "agora". This open area was located at the center of a city, and the citizens of ancient Greece gathered there to do shopping, listen to public announcements and speeches, look for employment, and get together for debates. They debated about such topics as biology, politics, ethics[20], and philosophy. These debates formed the foundation of Western thought, science, and politics.

In modern day Western society, the debate style of communication can be seen everywhere. Not only is this style of communication seen in formal situations such as government sessions, academic conference[21] presenta-

---

14　participant: 参加者
15　intentionally: わざと, 故意に
16　sought: seek の過去形；seek: 捜し求める
17　modify: 部分修正する
18　evolve: 進化する
19　trace back: 遡る
20　ethics: 倫理

tions, scientific journal articles, and court trials[22], but it is also seen in everyday conversations with friends and family. Debating is even an organized event, and many university debate teams participate in competitions. In the West, being able to express your opinion is considered important, and being able to make a persuasive[23] argument is considered to be a valuable skill and a sign of intelligence (Barnlund 1975: 89). In Western culture, it is natural to ask questions during a university lecture, and to even disagree with what the professor is saying. It is believed that by disagreeing and then discussing, the student will gain a much deeper understanding of the information, and thus questions tend to be encouraged.

Although debating is a common practice in Western culture, it is avoided[24] in many others, including Japanese culture. Debating is avoided in Japanese culture because disagreeing with someone, particularly in public, is believed to result in that person losing face[25] (De Mente 2008, 賀川洋 1997). In Japanese culture, protecting the face of the person you are talking to is very important, much more so than trying to improve an idea and express your own opinion. For example, if a student were to disagree with what a professor was saying during a lecture, then the professor would lose face and possibly even dislike the student.

Although Japanese culture does not value the act of arguing, Japanese speakers still disagree with each other. However, instead of disagreeing directly, they tend to look for ways to express their disagreement indirectly[26] (De Mente 2008, 賀川洋 1997). One common strategy is to use expres-

---

21　academic conference: 学会
22　court trial: 裁判
23　persuasive: 説得力のある
24　avoid: 避ける
25　lose face: メンツを失う
26　indirectly: 間接的に

sions such as「少し考えさせて下さい」. Here is an example of the use of this phrase in a post on the website 教えて!goo[27]:

> 20歳男です。最近、すごーく奥手の女性（同じ会社の人で1コ上）と話をする機会がありました。何度か話をしていたら雰囲気・趣味等が似ていて、彼氏もいないということで（本人から聞きました）「今度、一緒に映画でも観にいきませんか？ 無理にとは言いませんが…」と誘ったところ（動揺）⇒女の子「いつですか？」私「都合のいい日でいいですよ」⇒（やはり動揺）⇒女の子「考えさせて下さい」
> というやり取りになってしまいました。その女の子の動揺は奥手のせいなのか、見て直ぐに分かりました。嫌そうな表情ではなかったのですが、やはり「考えさせて下さい」は柔らかく断ったということでしょうか？ 普通に私と喋る分には、私の話にも乗っかってくるので、嫌われてるわけではないと思うのですが…。

The phrase「少し考えさせて下さい」does not directly refuse[28] the invitation or idea, and thus prevents the other person from losing face. In fact, in Western society, a response of "let me think about it a bit" would often be seen as a positive response, particularly in response to a suggested new idea. The Western interpretation[29] of such a response is that some time is needed to think of problems and possible solutions, and that the idea will be discussed more in the near future with the intention[30] of improving it. In contrast, in Japan such a response is intended to kill the original idea by not talking about it again. This process is called 自然消滅 in Japanese.

So now that you understand the source of cultural miscommunication, go back to the story about Takahashi-san. What do you think Takahashi-san

---

27 教えて!goo: http://oshiete.goo.ne.jp/qa/5243064.html.
28 refuse: 断る，拒否する
29 interpretation: 解釈
30 intention: 意図

should do? I think he should do several things. First, he should learn about these cultural differences in communication so that he can identify[31] the source of the problem. Second, he should talk with his boss about intercultural communication, and explain that the Japanese style of communication is to avoid debating and disagreeing with colleagues[32]. This will help the boss realize that Takahashi-san has been trying to do the best job he can. Hopefully, the boss will become more understanding of the Japanese style of communication. Finally, Takahashi-san should promise to make an effort to debate more in the meetings, and then do so. This should restore[33] the boss's faith[34] in Takahashi-san, and repair the damaged relationship between them.

> *Check your understanding 5.1*
> Is disagreeing considered to be a good or bad practice in Western society? Why? What about Japanese society? Why?
> *Answer: Disagreeing is a considered to be a good practice in Western society. It is seen as a way to improve an idea. A person who is skillful at arguing is considered to be intelligent. In contrast, disagreeing is considered to be a bad practice in Japanese society. Arguing with someone, particularly in public, results in that person losing face.*

Apologizing

Another area of communication that is varies with cultures is apologizing.

31　identify: 不明の物事を明らかにする
32　colleague: 同僚
33　restore: 元に戻す
34　faith: 信用，信頼

Examples of Cultural Differences in Communication

In the previous chapter (page 65), I gave the example of answering your cell phone in the middle of a conversation with a friend. In Japan, it would not be unusual to give a light apology for the interruption in the conversation. In contrast, in Western culture an apology in this situation would be strange. Westerners tend to apologize much less frequently[35] and in fewer situations (Elwood 2001, 賀川洋 1997). Interrupting a conversation with a friend in order to answer a cell phone is not a situation in which a Westerner would apologize.

Here is another example from my own experience. I asked another professor to do a certain task for me right away. I made the request by sending an email to him, and he responded by email. Here is his response:

> I'm underprepared for 3 very different zemis[36] today, so I don't have time for this. I'll start it on the weekend.

This is the entire contents of the response; only his name has been omitted[37]. Notice that there is no apology, even though my request was refused (in that he did not do it right away, but waited until the weekend). This is another example of where apologizing is not necessary in Western culture. In contrast, I think that most Japanese would feel a strong obligation[38] to apologize after refusing to accept a request. The apology may be something light, such as 「ごめんね」 or it could be as formal as 「ご希望に添えず、申し訳ありません」.

There is, however, something else in the email response that is very important: an explanation of why the request could not be fulfilled[39] imme-

---

35　frequently: 頻繁に
36　zemis: 「ゼミ」の複数形
37　omit: 省く
38　obligation: 義務
39　fulfill: 実行する，果たす

diately. The professor wrote that he was very busy preparing for three zemi classes, and did not have time until the weekend. In Western culture, in many situations an explanation is provided instead of an apology. Note that Japanese culture is quite different: in many situations an apology is provided but an explanation is not (Elwood 2001, 賀川洋 1997). In fact, De Mente (2008), in his book about Japanese culture, says that apologizing is "standard practice during and after almost every conversation" (p. 93). In contrast to this, I think that in Western culture, giving an explanation is standard practice during and after almost every conversation. To give another example, recall the discussion of interrupting a conversation with a friend in order to answer your cell phone. I said that in this situation, Western cultural norms[40] are to give an explanation instead of an apology, and I gave the following as an example explanation: "That was my cousin. She called to cancel our lunch date."

Now let us compare the above email to another email message, this time from a Japanese student:

> I can't go to your office tomorrow. I'm sorry. I will come on Wednesday.

Again this is the entire contents of the message, other than the student's name. Note that the student has apologized, and has not given any explanation as to why he cannot come. Western communication style is the opposite: do not apologize and explain briefly why you cannot come.

> **Check your understanding 5.2**
> Complete the following sentence: An apology is to the Japanese as an _____ is to Westerners.
> *Answer: Explanation. The Japanese often apologize and seldom give an*

---

40 western cultural norms: 西欧文化の基準

Examples of Cultural Differences in Communication

> *explanation. In contrast, Westerners often explain and seldom apologize.*

Complimenting

Explanations are extremely effective in Western culture, and are expected in many situations. Inviting, refusing, congratulating, criticizing, praising, and so on, all come with explanations. I will give some examples of responding to a compliment with an explanation.

Here are two scenarios. Think of how you would respond in each situation. Soon after you start working at a company, you are invited out to karaoke with your new colleagues. You are quite good at karaoke because you have belonged to a 合唱倶楽部 since you were a young child. Naturally, people compliment you:「本当に歌が上手ですね。素晴らしかったです」. What is a culturally appropriate response[41] in this situation?

Compare the karaoke scenario with this scenario. You are a university student taking English communication classes. When you were younger, you lived in Singapore for two years. While living there, you learned English while playing with Singapore children. Although you are not fluent, you can speak with confidence. After you gave a small presentation in English class, the teacher compliments you: "Wow! That was really good. You speak with such confidence." What is a culturally appropriate response in this situation?

The culturally appropriate response in the first scenario is to deny[42] your ability with expressions such as「いいえ、下手です」and「それほどではありません」. The compliment is denied because Japanese culture values humil-

---

41 a culturally appropriate response: 文化的に適切な答え
42 deny: 否認する

ity[43] (Elwood 2001, 賀川洋 1997, 八代京子 et al. 2001), as shown by the well-known saying: 「謙譲は美徳である」. What about in the second scenario? The culturally appropriate response in Western culture is to do the opposite: instead of denying the compliment, you accept the compliment and acknowledge[44] that it is true by saying words of gratitude[45] such as "thank you". Compliments are seldom[46] denied. However, saying thank you is often not enough. The key to accepting a compliment is the explanation. Westerners often give a brief explanation of how or why they are able to perform so well. For example, in response to a compliment about your singing ability, you could say, "Thank you. I have always loved singing and have been singing since I was a child." Similarly, in response to a compliment about your English ability, you could say, "You really think so? I lived in Singapore for two years when I was younger."

Check your understanding 5.3

What are the two parts of a response to a compliment in Western culture?

Answer: Gratitude and explanation.

■ Connections with the debate style of communication

To summarize[47] this section so far, apologies and compliments in Japanese and Western cultures are very different. When refusing a request, Westerners tend not to say sorry and tend to give an explanation instead of apologizing. In contrast, the Japanese frequently apologize and seldom give

---

43　humility: 謙遜
44　acknowledge: 認める
45　gratitude: 感謝
46　seldom: 稀に
47　summarize: 要約する

Examples of Cultural Differences in Communication

an explanation along with the apology. When responding to a compliment, Westerners tend to accept the compliment with words of gratitude but also give some explanation, whereas the Japanese tend to deny the compliment, and seldom give an explanation.

These differences in apologies and compliments are not independent of each other; they reflect the more general cultural difference called *debate style* that I described earlier in the chapter (page 80). Recall[48] that in Western culture, explaining your opinions, actions, or decisions is very important. This is also true when apologizing and when responding to a compliment: an explanation is important. When Westerners receive an apology, they want to understand the logic behind the opinion, action, or decision. Similarly, responding to a compliment with an explanation allows everyone to understand the logic behind why a person is good at singing or at speaking English. This is a key point for successful intercultural communication between Westerners and Japanese, and it is worth repeating one more time.

> Explanations are a very important part of communication in Western culture.

Eye contact

In this section and the following section, two examples of paralinguistic communication are introduced. Recall from the discussion in Chapter 1 (page 8) that the paralinguistic component of a message is a part of nonverbal communication. Examples of paralinguistic components include

---

48 recall: 思い出す

rate of speech, gestures, length of pauses, and loudness. In this section, I introduce eye contact. In the next section, I will talk about touching.

Eye contact refers to how often and for how long you look another person directly in the eyes. In every culture, looking someone directly in the eyes has meaning. However, this meaning differs greatly from one culture to the next.

Let's begin by discussing eye contact in Western culture. Westerners interpret[49] short eye contact by a speaker as nervousness[50] and perhaps even that the speaker is lying. Short eye contact by a listener is seen as a sign that he or she is not interested in what is being said. In the west, short eye contact is, in general, seen as undesirable[51] behavior (賀川洋 1997).

On the other hand, Western culture values long eye contact. It is seen as a sign that the speaker is confident, or that the listener is interested in what is being said. Long eye contact is important when giving an apology, as it is seen as a sign that the speaker is sincere[52] about the apology and that he has reflected on his actions[53]. In general, long eye contact is considered to be very desirable behavior (賀川洋 1997).

The author of a website[54] called the *Art of Seduction*[55] makes this point very strongly. The web site contains advice on how men can easily talk with women. One of the website's articles[56] is titled "Five small changes that will drastically[57] improve your game." It gives the five pieces of advice

---

49 interpret: 解釈する
50 nervousness: 不安，臆病，神経質
51 undesirable: 望ましくない
52 sincere: 誠実な，正直な
53 reflected on his actions: 行動を反省した
54 Art of Seduction: http://www.artofseductions.com/
55 seduction: 誘惑；the art of seduction: 口説き方虎の巻
56 article: 記事
57 drastically: 徹底的に

for men trying to appear more attractive to women. At the top of the list is eye contact. Here is what the article says:[58]

> One of the sexiest things a guy can do is meet a woman's eyes. There is a saying, "the eyes are the window to the soul[59]," yet so few men feel capable of revealing their souls to build a better connection with a woman by looking her in the eyes. When you look deep into a woman's eyes without feeling embarrassed or ashamed[60], a powerful tension[61] is built between the two of you. Women will feel it just as strongly as men. Strong eye contact can build attraction between two people of the opposite sex. A simple trick to help you maintain[62] eye contact is to practice on strangers with the goal that you will not look away until you can tell what color eyes the person has.

This article claims that if a man looks in to the eyes of a woman, then she will feel attracted[63] to him. What do you think?

Interestingly, eye contact in Japanese culture is very different from that of Western culture. In Japanese culture, short eye contact by a speaker is interpreted as a sign of humility and of respect for the listener. Therefore, this is seen as desirable behavior (賀川洋 1997).

On the other hand, Japanese culture interprets long eye contact as aggressive behavior, and a sign of insolence[64] or rebellion[65]. There was a

---

58 The original content has been edited to make it easier to read.
59 soul: 魂
60 feel ashamed: 恥じている
61 tension: 緊張
62 maintain: 保持する，継続する
63 feel attracted: 魅力を感じる
64 insolence: 傲慢，無礼
65 rebellion: 反抗

point in time when a commoner[66] could be killed for maintaining long eye contact with a samurai (賀川洋 1997). Similarly, long eye contact must be avoided in Japanese culture when giving an apology.

These cultural differences about eye contact are summarized in Table 5.1. It is easy to imagine situations in which these differences become a source of intercultural miscommunication. Consider again the story of Takahashi-san, the Japanese employee working for an American boss. Takahashi-san seems like the type of person who would not make eye contact with his boss while his boss is talking to him. Furthermore, his boss seems like the type of person who would misunderstand this.

	Long Eye Contact	Short Eye Contact
Western Culture	confident（自信がある） reflected on mistakes （反省する） interested（興味がある）	lack of interest （興味が無い） lying（嘘をつく）
Japanese Culture	impudent（生意気） rebellious（反抗する）	humble and respectful （謙遜である） apologetic （申し訳ないと思う）

Table 5.1: The meaning of different lengths of eye contact in Westen and Japanese culture

Check your understanding 5.4
Does the following situation require long eye contact or short eye contact: showing respect for the speaker in Western culture?
Answer: Long eye contact. In general, in Western culture long eye contact is positive while short eye contact is negative.

66　commoner: 平民，庶民

Examples of Cultural Differences in Communication

Touching

Another type of nonverbal communication is touching. Depending on the culture, touching is used as a way to:
- greet someone you meet for the first time
- greet someone you have not seen in a long time
- show admiration[67] for an achievement
- show friendship, intimacy[68], and group membership
- show toughness

The act of touching varies[69] greatly from one culture to the next. Some cultures value touching, and it is used as an essential part of communication. Members of other cultures avoid touching while communicating. Communication in Romance cultures such as French and Brazilian culture involves lots of touching, communication in Japanese and Chinese culture involves very little touching, and communication in American culture lies between these two extremes[70] (賀川洋 1997, von Raffler-Engel 1996). These differences are seen very clearly when members of these different culture interact[71] with each other on a daily basis[72]. In some cultures touching the person you are talking to is a normal part of conversation.

Cultural differences in touching are easily observable[73] when two people greet each other, for example, after having not seen each other for some

---

67 admiration: 賞賛の気持ち，感嘆
68 intimacy: 親しいこと，親密
69 vary: 変化する
70 extreme: 極端
71 interact: 交流する
72 on a daily basis: 日ごろ
73 observable: 観察できる

period of time. In many cultures, a kiss is part of the greeting. Exactly how this is done and who does it varies greatly from one culture to the next. For example, in the Romance cultures people often do what is known as kissing cheeks. This is the act of pressing[74] one of your cheeks to the cheek of the person you are greeting, and then switching sides and pressing the other cheek. In some cultures, such as French culture, such a greeting is appropriate regardless of the age, sex, or how well the greeters know each other. In other cultures, cheek kissing is normally only done between members of the opposite sex. Besides kissing, other actions that take place during a greeting include touching the upper arm, and the ubiquitous[75] hand shake. In contrast, Japanese people tend not to touch at all when greeting someone.

Kissing during a greeting in English-speaking cultures is rare. A child's relatives of the opposite sex may kiss the child once on the cheek. Also, in large cities such as New York and Toronto, some young adults may greet close friends of the opposite sex with a kiss on the cheek. However, unlike in French culture, even in large cities kissing between members of the same sex is extremely rare, particularly between two men.

These cultural differences in greetings are seen when world leaders greet each other. Table 5.2 lists the amount of touching that took place when the American President Obama greeted various leaders for the first time, as seen in the television news coverage[76] of the occasions. Comparing the number of touching actions performed during the greetings shows a striking[77] contrast[78]. Much more touching occurred during greetings with the

---

74　press: 押し付ける
75　ubiquitous: 遍在する，あらゆるところに存在する
76　coverage: 取材
77　striking: 著しい
78　contrast: 対象

French and Brazilian presidents than with the Chinese president and the Canadian prime minister.

Date and Location	The Other Person	Touching Actions Performed
February 19, 2009 Ottawa, Canada	Canadian Prime Minister Harper	• shaking with one hand
April 3, 2009 Strasbourg, France	French President Sarkozy	• shaking with two hands • patting on the back • hugging • kissing cheeks • poking chest
November 24, 2009 Washington, U.S.A.	Indian Prime Minster Singh	• shaking with one hand • shaking with two hands
January 19, 2011 Washington, U.S.A.	Chinese president Hu	• shaking with one hand
March 19, 2011 Brasilia, Brazil	Brazilian President Lula	• shaking with one hand • shaking with two hands • touching arm

Table 5.2: The various touching actions that were performed during greetings between several world leaders and President Obama

Perhaps the greetings reflect political[79] attitudes, but this explanation is unlikely. Canada and the United States are considered to be politically very close to each other (for example, Canada was the first place President Obama visited outside of the United States), and yet their greeting had the smallest amount of touching seen in Table 5.2: a handshake with one hand.

A better explanation for the differences in the amount of touching during the greetings is that it reflects differences in cultures. Both Chinese and Canadian culture tend to have less touching than French and Brazilian culture, and therefore more touching occurred when President Obama greeted the French and Brazilian presidents than when he greeted the

---

79　political: 政治の

Canadian prime minister and the Chinese president.

> *Check your understanding 5.5*
>
> Japan is not listed as one of the locations in Table 5.2. If Japan was added to the table, what amount of touching during the greeting do you think would be appropriate?
>
> Answer: *Although Japanese people do not normally greet each other by shaking hands, it is not completely unheard of in Japan, and is done when greeting non-Japanese. Most likely, the greeting would be similar as that with the Chinese or Canadian leaders: shaking hands with one hand.*

■ The role of touching in Western sports

One situation in which communication through touching occurs very frequently is during games of competitive team sports such as soccer, baseball, and football. During the games, teammates frequently touch each other as a way of congratulating after scoring a point or comforting a player who missed a difficult shot. Following are some examples of the types of touching that occurs between teammates:

- high five[80] (both players raise their right hands above their heads and slap their hands together)
- fist[81] bump (both players make a fist with their right hand and bump their knuckles[82] together)
- butt[83] slap (one player slaps the buttocks of another player)
- bear hug (one player embraces[84] another player in a hug and then lifts that player

---

80 high five: ハイタッチ
81 fist: 拳
82 knuckle: 指関節
83 butt: 「buttocks」の省略，人の尻

off of the ground)

This touching occurs most often immediately after scoring. The scoring player is quickly surrounded by other teammates, and the touching takes place between the scoring player and the other teammates.

Sociologists have wondered why teammates touch each other so much. Research on professional American basketball players (Kraus et al. 2010) has shown that touching between players is connected to how well both the individual player and the team as a whole does. Teams with players that touch frequently seem to perform better than teams with players that do not touch so often. This is a surprising result. How does touching a teammate help him play basketball better? The researchers point out that touching helps people build trust and reduce stress. For example, a crying baby is comforted[85] when the mother holds the child in her arms[86]. Building trust and reducing stress are important when playing competitive team sports, as they lead to improved performance.

Basketball players are not the only players who do so much touching. In fact, it is a common behavior seen in other competitive team sports, such as professional baseball and football. This touching among American teammates occurs in spite of the fact that in general, in Western culture, touching does not occur, particularly between males. However, the culture of team sports takes priority over[87] the more general culture of society, and touching is a very important part of communication during competitive events.

84　embrace: 抱きしめる
85　comfort: 慰める
86　hold in arms: 抱く
87　take priority over: に優先する

Key points for Chapter 5

- ▶ The debate style of communication emphasizes the following:
  - explaining your opinions, actions, or decisions clearly
  - asking questions about other's ideas or opinions
  - disagreeing with others
  - building up an idea through argument
  - changing the original idea in response to criticism
- ▶ The debate style of communication is common among Westerners, and for them the ability to make a persuasive[88] argument is considered a valuable skill.
- ▶ The debate style of communication is avoided by the Japanese people, as disagreeing with someone openly will cause that person to lose face.
- ▶ Japanese people use nonverbal and paralinguistic components of the message in order to disagree with someone.
- ▶ Westerners tend to apologize much less than Japanese people and to give an explanation instead of apologizing. Japanese people frequently apologize and seldom give an explanation along with the apology.
- ▶ In Western culture, long eye contact has positive meanings, whereas in Japanese culture, long eye contact has negative meanings.
- ▶ The amount of touching done during communication varies according to the culture.
- ▶ Touching is an important part of communication between teammates in competitive sports, as it helps build trust and reduce stress.

---

88 persuasive: 説得力のある

Examples of Cultural Differences in Communication

PRACTICE QUESTIONS

Q 5.1 This chapter discussed several examples of communication differences between Japanese and Western culture. These are examples of hidden culture, and therefore take some effort to master. Of the topics discussed in this chapter, which do you think is the most difficult for Japanese people to master? Explain why you think that.

Q 5.2 Rank the following cultures in order from the most amount of touching to the least amount of touching:

American   Chinese   Japanese   Spanish

Q 5.3 a. Give a response to the compliment "your English is so good" that is appropriate in Western culture.

b. What do you think would happen if in response to "your English is so good," you replied, "yes, it is," without any explanation?

Q 5.4 The following are two email messages. One of them was written by a Japanese person, and the other was written by a Westerner. Which email was written by the Japanese person and which email was written by the Westerner? How do you know?

> I forgot to mention[89] it, I think, but this Monday night may not work[90] for me; I'll be coming back from Fujisan that day.

> I'm sorry, but I can't make it[91] tomorrow.

---
89 mention: について言及する，ちょっと触れる
90 not work: same as "not work out"；駄目だ

| Q 5.5 | Observe[92] how Japanese players in a competitive team sport such as baseball congratulate each other after scoring. Do they do any touching? If so, how frequently, and what type of touching do they do?

| Q 5.6 | Why do players of competitive team sports who do a lot of touching perform better than players who do not do a lot of touching?

| Q 5.7 | Read the following story[93] about a Japanese exchange student in the United States, and then answer the following questions.

> This story is about a Japanese exchange student named Ikeda Junko. She was an exchange student at an American university. During her first semester, she took only English as a Second Language courses. However, during her second semester, she took regular university courses. Junko was particularly interested in language and culture, and so she eagerly enrolled for a course titled "Speech and Communication". However, things did not go so well. Although Junko could follow what the instructor was saying, when classroom discussion between classmates began, she could barely keep up with the fast pace of the conversation. She certainly was not capable of confidently expressing her own opinion in such an environment. As a result, Junko felt very uncomfortable in the class, and had a difficult time talking with the her classmates.
>
> The second last lecture of the semester was a formal debate. The students, after a typically enthusiastic discussion, decided on the topic

---

91 can't make it: 参加できない
92 observe: 観察する
93 This story is based on pages 93 to 95 of 久米 & 長谷川 (2007).

Examples of Cultural Differences in Communication

of gay marriage. The class of thirty students was systematically divided into two groups based on the alphabetical order of their last names. The first group was to support gay marriage, while the second group was to oppose gay marriage. Members of each group took turns presenting an argument for or against gay marriage. Junko was assigned to the first group.

Junko hoped to use this opportunity to restore her reputation[94], and went to work preparing for the debate. She researched several key points for the argument in support of gay marriage and prepared notes. However, when the actual debated started, her American classmates quickly made all of the points that Junko had so diligently[95] prepared. In the end, the debate ended without Junko even saying a word.

On the last lecture of the semester, Junko went to class as usual. However, she immediately felt that something was different. Her classmates seemed to have suddenly become very cold toward her, and even those classmates that at least used to smile at her no longer smiled at her. The classmates seemed to be angry at her. The last lecture ended with Junko having no idea what she did to cause such resentment[96] from her classmates.

  a. Why did Junko have such a difficult time in the class? Why were the classmates angry with Junko? Use your knowledge of hidden culture (page 65), the debate style of communication (page 80), and out-group bias (page 28) in your answer.

  b. What do you think Junko should have done once she realized

---

94　reputation: 評判，世評
95　diligently: 精を出して，念入りに
96　resentment: 憤慨，怒り

that her American classmates had said all of the key points that she had prepared?

6 Culturally Dependent Communication Styles

The last chapter introduced several cultural differences in communication. These were differences in specific[1] situations: disagreeing, apologizing, and so on. This chapter introduces more cultural differences in communication. However, the differences introduced in this chapter are more general than those introduced in the previous chapter. I call these general differences **communication styles**. In the previous chapter, I already introduced one communication style: the debate style (page 80). This chapter introduces the following styles: *high context, low context, group,* and *individual*. Finally, the chapter ends by with the idea of social power distance.

High context and low context styles

Once again, I begin with a story in order to introduce the topic:[2]

> Keiko is a Japanese exchange student who is attending an American university for one year, and living in Dallas, Texas. Keiko lives in a student apartment with an American roommate named Jane. Keiko is

---

1 specific: 特定の
2 This story is based on page 39 of 八代京子 et al. (2001).

a serious student who works hard. Of course, taking university courses in English is stressful, and Keiko is a little bit anxious. At the time of this story, Keiko had a mid-term test the next day, and she wanted to study hard. However, she could not concentrate because Jane had just arrived back home, and was listening to music in her bedroom. The music was not loud, but Keiko could hear it clearly in her room, and it was getting[3] on her nerves. She decided to talk to Jane. This is the conversation that they had:

    Keiko: Hi, Jane.
    Jane: Hey, Keiko, what's up?
    Keiko: Tomorrow I have a big test.
    Jane: Oh, yeah? But, hey, you're always studying, right? I think you'll do fine.
    Keiko: Actually, I got a bad score on my test, so I have to study very hard!
    Jane: Oh, that sucks.
    Keiko: So I must concentrate and study hard, you know?
    Jane: Yeah… good luck on the test!

At this point, one of Jane's friends called Jane, interrupting the conversation. Jane turned down the music so Keiko went back to her room to begin studying again. However, much to Keiko's surprise, after twenty minutes Jane turned up the music again to the same volume as before. Keiko was very angry with Jane for ignoring her situation, but she had no idea what she should do.

Although Keiko was very angry with Jane, it is important to understand that Jane was not intentionally[4] trying to be confrontational[5]. In fact, Jane

---

3 getting on a person's nerves: 癪に障る
4 intentionally: わざと，故意に

undoubtedly[6] has no idea that Keiko was angry or even why she could be angry. This misunderstanding is an example of intercultural miscommunication. Keiko thinks that she asked Jane to turn down her music and be quiet. However, Jane thinks that Keiko was just chatting, and did not consider the conversation to be a request to turn down the music. She turned down the music so that she could talk on the phone with her friend. However, once the telephone conversation was over, there was no reason to keep the music volume down.

The source of the misunderstanding is the words, "So I must concentrate and study hard, you know?" The verbal[7] component of the message is the words, "I must concentrate and study hard." However, there is a nonverbal component to the message as well. It is the request, "could you please turn down the music?" Jane was listening to Keiko, but she was really only listening to the verbal component. Therefore, she missed the nonverbal component.

■ High context style of communication

Keiko is using a style of communication known as high context style. **High context style** of communication emphasizes[8] the nonverbal component. In cultures that use the high context style of communication, such as Japanese culture, the speaker expects the listener to understand the non-spoken message based on the context. That is, the communication style makes high (i.e., frequent) use of the context, and hence[9] the name of the communication style is high context style. Recall from Chapter 1 (page 10) that the

---

5   confrontational: 対決的な
6   undoubtedly: きっと…に違いない
7   Verbal component and nonverbal component were introduced in Chapter 1, page 7.
8   emphasize: 強調する
9   hence: そのゆえに，したがって

context of a message is the environment in which the communication takes place. This includes the speaker, the addressee, the relationship between the two people, the situation, and so on. This idea of using context in order to understand the nonverbal message is illustrated[10] by the Japanese phrase 「空気を読む」. In this story, Keiko expects Jane to understand her request from her description of the situation: she has a test the next day and must study hard.

In high context cultures members of the same in-group (see Chapter 2, page 28) are able to communicate complex messages with few words. Members of the same in-group have the similar cultural backgrounds, experiences, expectations, and assumptions. Addressees use this common set of values to infer[11] the nonverbal component of the message. The paralinguistic component of the message is also very important, because it contains clues to the nonverbal message.

Following are some more examples of high context communication:

Example One

> A high school dance circle is preparing for the 文化祭. They decide that they want to use more space than they originally planned. However, they need to get permission from the teachers. A 先輩 says to a 後輩,「じゃぁ、この事、なんとかしておいてください」.

Example Two

> Yamada-san's parents live on a farm. He occasionally helps out on the farm. Every time he visits his parents, he receives fresh vegetables that were grown in the fields. One day he told his neighbor this, and the neighbor replied, "You are lucky to be able to get fresh vegetables. The

---

10 A is illustrated by B: A が B によって説明される
11 infer: 推測する,推量する

> vegetables in the grocery store are never fresh." After that, Yamada-san sometimes gives some vegetables to his neighbor, even though his neighbor never asked for the vegetables.

Example Three

> A husband and wife are taking a trip by car. The husband is driving. He decides to stop briefly to buy a beverage[12] from a convenience store. Even though his wife did not ask him to do so, he also buys a beverage for her. The husband uses his knowledge of his wife's preferences[13] to pick a drink for her.

In the first example, the verbal message is not clear. Regardless, the 後輩 understands exactly what is being asked. She uses the context and the previous conversations to understand the request. In the second example, Yamada-san infers the request for vegetables from his neighbor's words: "The vegetables in the grocery store are never fresh." The third example dose not even have a verbal message. However, the husband infers his wife's desire for a beverage from their similar cultural backgrounds and experiences together as a couple.

Many cultures around the world prefer a high context style of communication. Following is a list of some of the cultures that prefer a high context style of communication (Copeland & Griggs 1986, Hofstede et al. 2010):

- East Asian (Chinese, Japanese, Korean)
- Romance (French, Italian, Spanish, Portuguese, Latin American)
- Russian
- Arab
- Filipino[14]

---

12 beverage: 飲み物
13 preferences: 好み

- Indian

In these cultures, the nonverbal component plays an important role in communication. Note that Japanese culture is considered to be a high context culture.

In addition, some situations tend to use a higher context style of communication than other situations. These situations involve people who know each other very well or people who perform the same activity together on a regular basis. Their common experiences together allows them to infer nonverbal messages. Here are some examples of situations that tend to use a higher context style:

- a group of close friends talking together
- a family eating dinner together
- a customer drinking in a whiskey bar that he goes to regularly after work
- a nurse and a doctor working together in a clinic

In these situations, the people speak with each other so often that they know what the other person wants without asking. Consider the example of the customer who drinks whiskey in a whiskey bar. These bars tend to be very small places run by a middle-aged women (ママさん). These women know their customers' favorite snacks and drinks. They also know their personalities and can guess if their customers are in good moods. Note that these types of high context style situations occur in low context style cultures as well as in high context style cultures.

Check your understanding 6.1

In the first example of high context style that I gave, a 先輩 says to a 後輩,「じゃぁ、この事、なんとかしておいてください」. What is the verbal component of this message? What is the nonverbal component of this message?

---

14   Filipino: フィリピン人の

> Answer: The verbal message is 「この事、なんとかしておいてください」, and the nonverbal message is "Please ask the teachers for more space".

■ Low context style of communication

In the above story about Keiko and Jane, Jane did not comprehend[15] the nonverbal component of Keiko's message. This happened because Jane is using a style of communication called low context style. **Low context style** of communication emphasizes the verbal component and de-emphasizes the nonverbal component. In this type of communication, all important information tends to be stated[16] explicitly[17], and therefore it is not necessary to 「空気を読む」.

In the above story about Keiko and Jane, Jane used the verbal components of the messages to understand what Keiko was saying. Keiko never explicitly stated that she was having a hard time studying. Therefore, Jane never understood that there was the problem. She was unable to 「空気を読む」 because the low context communication style focuses on the contents of the verbal component. Keiko should have explicitly stated that she was having a hard time studying in the verbal component of her message.

Following are some more examples of low context communication:

Example One

> In the United States and Canada, apartment buildings often have a laundry room in the basement. Laundry rooms have several washing machines and dryers for doing laundry. Normally, people put their laundry in a machine, start it, leave and then return an hour later. While

---

15　comprehend: 理解する
16　state: 述べる
17　explicitly: 明白に

> I was living in such a building, I accidently forgot to return and left a load[18] of laundry in a washing machine for more than a day. When I finally returned to get my laundry, I found a note on the machine. It said, "Please do not leave laundry in the washing machine. Other people want to use it too." After that, I was more careful about picking up my laundry.

Example Two

> Asahi Breweries released a new 発泡酒 called 一番麦 in March, 2011. The front of the can stated「麦100％　麦芽・大麦・スピリッツ(大麦)を使用，ホップ使用量(0.5％未満)を除く」.

Example Three

> A low-level manager at the Honda plant[19] in Alliston, Canada gave a tour to a senior Japanese Honda employee who was visiting from Japan. The manager explained in great detail how the plant manufactures cars, even though the Japanese employee already has a very good understanding of the entire process.

In the first example, the problem (I left clothes in a washing machine for too long) was explicitly stated in the note left on the washing machine. In the second example, the description of the ingredients[20] used to make the beer is very explicit. In the third example, the Canadian manager explains in great detail about the plant.

Several cultures around the world prefer a low context style of communication. The following list shows some of the cultures that use a low context

---

18 a load of laundry: 一回分の洗濯物
19 plant: 工場
20 ingredients: 材料，成分

style of communication (Copeland & Griggs 1986, Hofstede et al. 2010):
- German, Austrian, Swiss
- Scandinavian (Denmark, Norway, and Sweden)
- English
- Irish
- Israeli

In these cultures, the nonverbal component of communication is not as important as it is in high context cultures.

In addition, some situations tend to require a low context style more than other situations. In these situations, maintaining the same message regardless of context is important, perhaps because the speaker and the addressee are strangers. In other cases, the message being communicated is public, or the communication is based on a set of rules. Here are some examples of situations that use a low context style of communication:
- asking a stranger for directions
- going through a security checkpoint at an airport
- paying for a purchase at a cash register[21] in a store
- a soccer referee gives a player a yellow card
- a teacher gives instructions to the class at the beginning of a test

The communication in these situations occurs between strangers, or the communication is based on a set of rules or laws. In these situations, it is important that no misunderstandings occur. Therefore, high context communication is avoided.

Check your understanding 6.2

Based on the combination of culture and situation, which of the following situations is the lowest context and which is the highest context?

a. asking a stranger for directions in Japan

---

21 cash register: レジ

> b. asking a stranger for directions in the United States
> c. a nurse and a doctor working together in Japan
> d. a nurse and a doctor working together in the United States
>
> *Answer: Asking for directions is a low context style situation and the United States is a low context style culture. Thus, asking for directions in the United States is the lowest context style situation. Similary, a doctor and a nurse working together is a high context style situation, and Japan is a high context style culture. Thus, a doctor and a nurse working together in Japan is the highest context style situation.*

■ Connecting context style and debate style

An important link exists between context style and debate style. (Debate style was introduced on page 80.) That link is politeness. Recall from the discussion of the debate style that the Japanese tend to avoid disagreeing with another person directly. As part of that discussion, I gave the example of 「少し考えさせて下さい」. As I mentioned, the reason why direct disagreement is avoided in Japanese culture is because it causes the other person to lose face. In other words, it is rude. The solution is to use high context communication to disagree. You should now realize that 「少し考えさせて下さい」 is an excellent example of high context communication. That is, the speaker expects the listener to understand the non-spoken message based on the context (in this case, the nonverbal message is 「遠慮します」). Thus, using a high context style of communication when disagreeing and debating an idea prevents the other person from losing face, and therefore is considered to be polite.

Does this link between context style and debate style also exist[22] in Western culture? Yes, it does. As I discussed in the section on debate style

---

22 exist: 存在する

in the previous chapter (page 80), Westerners disagree with each other directly. However, they still manage to save the other person's face. This is done by providing explanations when they disagree. You should now realize that both disagreement and explanation are examples of the low context style of communication. Thus, a strong link exists between the debate style and the context style communication.

Group style and individual style communication

The next topic is group style communication. I will once again begin the topic with a story. The main character in this story is Takahashi-san's boss. His name is Bob. We have already met Bob in the story that appears on page 78.

> Bob is the president of an American-affiliated company[23] in Tokyo. He has been living in Tokyo for about one year now, and is getting used to his life in Japan. He is the father of a five-year-old girl. Every morning at 8:15, he brings her to an international kindergarten[24] near his house. The school has about 80 students. The number of Japanese and non-Japanese students are almost the same. Every morning Bob talks to some of the other parents as they drop off their children at the school.
> However, there is one strange thing that Bob cannot understand. When he walks his daughter to the school, he often crosses paths[25] with

---

23 American-affiliated company: 日米の合併企業
24 kindergarten: 幼稚園
25 cross paths: 道を交えた，会う

other Japanese parents who also take their children to the school. When Bob meets these other Japanese parents on the street, they always say 「おはようございます」 to him, even if they do not know him. However, when he crosses paths with Japanese people who are not parents of children at the school, they almost always ignore him. In contrast, when Bob crosses paths with Westerners he does not know, sometimes they say "Good morning," and sometimes they do not. Whether or not the other Westerner is also a parent of the child attending the school does not seem to be so important. This is summarized in Table 6.1.

Bob observed this pattern of morning greetings, but he does not know what to make of it[26]. He cannot understand why there are differences between Japanese people and Western people.

Parent of child at the school?	Japanese	Westerner
yes	often	sometimes
no	almost never	sometimes

Table 6.1: How often a person greets Bob, based on nationality and parent status

The pattern that Bob observed comes from a fundamental[27] difference between Japanese culture and Western culture: Japanese culture emphasizes group style communication whereas Western culture does not. When people use **group style communication**, they tend to:

1. consider themselves to be members of several groups, such as their extended family and the group of people with whom they work
2. value the group more than the individual

---

26 what to make of it: どう理解するか
27 fundamental: 基本的な

Let us consider each of these points in turn.

The first point states that people consider themselves to be members of groups. Perhaps the most important of these groups is the family. As children grow up, they learn that their brothers, sisters, and parents, as well as their aunts, uncles, cousins and grandparents form[28] a single group. Some other groups in a person's life might be the company which they work for, the sports team which they belong to, or the school which they attend.

Of course, people in non-group-based cultures also belong to groups such as their family and their workplace. The difference is that in group-based cultures, group membership is very important. It often plays a role in determining a person's behavior, including communication. In a non-group-based culture, group membership much less frequently determines a person's behavior.

The second point states that the group is more important than the individual. This point is described in the Japanese proverb[29] 「出る杭は打たれる」. This proverb suggests that a person who stand out from the group because of their actions, personality, etc., will not be liked by the group. As another example, consider the way that a Japanese person introduces himself. The name of the group is introduced first and the person's name is introduced last. A junior high school student calling a friend's house may introduce himself as 「もしもし、天満中学校、三年二組の山田太郎です」. This pattern is seen in many different cases, such as on a Japanese business card, or in the way an address is written on an envelope, with the 宛名 written after the 住所. In Western society, the group is seldom mentioned, and when it is, it appears after the person's name. Similarly, in response to the request, "Tell me about yourself," people from a group-based culture

---

28   form: 構成する
29   proverb: ことわざ，格言

will speak about the groups which they belong to. For example, when giving a self-introduction, Japanese tend to mention who their friends are more often than Westerners (Ip & Bond 1995). In contrast, people from a non-group-based culture tend to speak more about their own personal characteristics, such as their personalities, and emphasize their distinctiveness[30] (Nisbett 2006).

This second point, that is, that the group is more important than the individual, is important in Japanese culture. Therefore, Japanese culture values conformity[31] and similarity more than uniqueness and individuality. This feeling is so strong that, for example, when an athlete on a team is asked during an interview about an outstanding performance, the athlete often denies[32] such a performance, and she claims that she played no better than anyone else on the team (De Mente 2008, Elwood 2001, 賀川洋 1997).

The next section gives a detailed example of this point. However, let us first return to the story of Bob. The Japanese parents of students attending the international school, as members of a group-based culture, tend to view people as members of groups. In the case of the Japanese parents, they see themselves as members of a group of people who have something in common: they are parents of children who attend the same school. Because they are members of the same group, they tend to greet each other in the morning. In contrast, the Japanese people who are not parents of children who attend the school do not have any reason to consider Bob to be a member of the same group. Therefore they do not have a reason to say "good morning" to him. On the other hand, this idea of a group is not as important to Westerners. This is why no relationship exists between parent status and greetings for Westerners in Table 6.1. Rather, the individual

---

30　distinctiveness: 独特性
31　conformity: 一致すること
32　deny: 否定する，否認する

personalities of the each person determines whether that person greets Bob when he passes by.

■ An example of a group: 指定校

In this section, I introduce an example of a group, the 指定校. I chose this example because, from an English-speaking Westerner's viewpoint, it is a little difficult to understand the logic behind it. The word, 指定校, refers to a special relationship that many Japanese universities have with some high schools. A high school involved in this type of a relationship with a university may nominate[33] a very small number of students, normally one or two, to a specific faculty[34] at the university. These nominated students receive different treatment with respect to gaining admission[35] to that faculty. For example, the nominated students often are only required to participate in an interview in a relaxed atmosphere. They are not required to take the grueling[36] written entrance exam.

However, there are restrictions[37]. The students must obtain a certain grade point average (GPA) in order to qualify for nomination. Furthermore, the exact requirement depends on which high school the student comes from. Four of these 指定校 for the 総合政策学部 at 関西学院大学 are given in Table 6.2. I replaced the names of the high schools with fictitious[38] names in order to protect their privacy.

---

33 nominate: 推薦する，指名する
34 faculty: 大学の学部
35 admission: 入学
36 grueling: へとへとに疲れさせる
37 restriction: 制限
38 fictitious: 偽りの，うその，本物でない

学校名（仮）	評定平均	2011年度募集人員
加和田高等学校	4.0	1
龍滝学園	3.5	2
宇忠任高等学校	3.5	1
西江戸高等学校	4.2	1

Table 6.2: Four of the 指定校 for 関西学院大学

Look at the last school in Table 6.2, 西江戸高等学校. This school has had the 指定校 relationship with 総合政策学部 for five or six years. Originally, two nominees[39] were accepted from this school. However, in 2010, the number of nominees was reduced from two to one. Then, in 2011, the required grade point average for the nominee was raised from 4.0 to 4.2. These changes make it more difficult for students attending that high school.

Why were these changes made? They were made because the graduates from the high school who were attending 総合政策学部 in the spring of 2011 were all perfoming poorly. Table 6.3 lists each student's current school year, grade point average, and the number of credits he or she has obtained so far. Other than the first year student who has not yet finish his or her first semester at the university, all of the students had poor GPAs.

学年	単位数	GPA	均点席次率
4 年	112	1.68	82.0%
4 年	100	1.15	94.1%
3 年	76	1.29	93.5%
3 年	28	0.46	97.4%
2 年	36	1.30	87.2%
2 年	40	1.24	90.6%
1 年			

Table 6.3: Grade point averages (GPA) for the 西江戸高等学校 students selected and sent to 関西学院大学 through the 指定校 system

---

[39] nominee: from the verb *nominate*; 指名された人

Reducing the number of nominees and raising the GPA requirements is not all that was done. The high school also received a letter that warned that, if the first year student also performs poorly, then the 指定校 relationship would be terminated[40].

From the perspective of a group-based culture, this seems logical. The students are a group. Their performance as a group will determine if the 指定校 relationship will end. However, from a Western perspective, the 指定校 system seems irrational[41]. Why should a very small number of students be treated differently from all of the other students? More importantly, why should the performance of one student determine the fate[42] of potential[43] students from that high school who might attend the university in the future? Perhaps it is a coincidence[44] that all of the current students are doing poorly. Perhaps, future students will be excellent. We will never know if future students will be excellent students if their opportunity to attend is denied. Although it is somewhat difficult to understand this system for a Western perspective, the 指定校 system seems to work very well because, in the end, Japanese culture is a group-based culture.

> *Check your understanding 6.3*
> Why is the story about 西江戸高等学校 difficult to understand from an English-speaking Western perspective?
> *Answer: English-speaking Western society is not a group-based society, and therefore emphasizes the abilities of the individual, not the group. Westerners have difficulty understanding how someone can be respon-*

---

40 terminate: 終わらせる，終結させる
41 irrational: 不合理な，理屈に合わない
42 fate: 運命
43 potential: 可能性のある，見込みのある
44 coincidence: 偶然

> sible for someone else's incompetence[45].

■ Group-based cultures around the world

So far, I have presented only two possibilities for cultures: group-based or non-group-based. In actuality, research has shown that cultures can also be between these two possibilities. For example, a culture could be between a group-based and a non-group-based culture (Hofstede et al. 2010). Researchers have published a list of 76 cultures and provided an index score[46] for each culture that indicates the extent[47] to which the culture is group-based. Table 6.4[48] is a selection taken from their list of cultures.

The values in the table indicate to what extent a culture emphasizes the group over the individual. Indonesia has the largest index score, indicating that Indonesian culture places a very strong emphasis on the group. In contrast, the United States has the lowest index score, indicating that American culture places a very strong emphasis on the individual, and group membership is not at all important. Notice that Japan is in the very middle. This shows that although I talk about Japanese culture as a group-based culture, relatively speaking[49], it is only somewhat group-based. Many cultures of the world are much more group-based than Japanese culture.

45　incompetence: 無能力
46　index score: 指数
47　extent: 程度
48　The data is taken from Table 4.1 of Hofstede et al. (2010). They present the data as an index of individualist-based culture. I have converted the scores to an index of group-based culture by subtracting the original values from 100.

Culturally Dependent Communication Styles

Culture	Group-Based Culture Index Score
United States	9
Canada	20
New Zealand	22
Italy	24
France	29
Finland	37
Israel	46
India	52
Japan	54
Arab countries	62
Philippines	68
Thailand	80
Korea	82
Taiwan	83
Indonesia	86

Table 6.4: Several cultures and their group-based culture index score

Check your understanding 6.4
In Table 6.4, the United States scores a value of 9. What does this value mean?
Answer: The number indicates the degree to which the culture of that country is group-based. A nine is a very low score. This means that the culture of the United States is not group-based at all.

■ More examples of group style communication

In the previous section, I introduced that idea that Japanese culture emphasizes the group and Western culture emphasizes the individual. These cultural differences influence the ways in which people communicate in

---

49 relatively speaking: 比較していえば

these cultures. Take, for example, the situation of a small group discussing where they should go to eat lunch. Non-Japanese are sometimes surprised by how long it can take such a group of Japanese people to make such a seemingly simple decision (Elwood 2001, 賀川洋 1997). The group debates all possibilities among themselves, and seeks a solution that everyone in the group feels comfortable with. In other words, the decision is made by the group as a whole. In contrast, in a non-group culture, often one or two people will do most of the decision-making, and the others will follow along.

In addition to the number of people involved in the decision, the actual way the decision is made also differs greatly. In a group-based culture such as Japan, people try to preserve harmony by avoiding confrontation, which can result in people losing face (De Mente 2008, 賀川洋 1997). To do this, people often hold back[50] their own opinions, even if they strongly disagree with the group's decision. In other words, the group's decision is more important than the feelings of an individual. This point is most likely connected to the point that Japanese people avoid debate style communication (discussed in Chapter 5, page 80). Rather, they use high context style communication (see the discussion of the link between the two styles discussed earlier in this chapter on page 112). These are both ways that make the group more important than the individual.

In contrast, Western culture emphasizes the individual's opinion. Recall from the discussion of debate style provided in the previous chapter (page 80), that in Western culture, when a person disagrees, he will voice his opinion and explain why he disagrees. Others are expected to act similarly, and decisions are made by individuals debating ideas. Thus, Westerners tend to use the debate style and a low context style of communication.

---

50 hold back: 遠慮する

■ Communication style and pronouns

Interestingly, cultural differences in context styles emerge in the grammars of languages, specifically the grammar of pronouns[51]. Kashima and Kashima (1998) looked at the relationship that exists between group-based culture and the grammar of pronouns. In Japanese, it is possible to omit[52] the pronoun in a sentence. For example, consider the following two sentences:

a.) 私はご飯を食べた
b.) ご飯を食べた

The first sentence includes the pronoun, 私. The second sentence is identical except that the pronoun, 私, has been omitted.

Kashima and Kashima found that a correlation[53] exists between omission of the first-person pronoun and the degree of group-based culture. Languages that allowed the omission of the first-person pronoun tend to score high on the group-based culture index.

Table 6.5 lists several languages, whether pronouns can be omitted, and each culture's group-based culture index score. This table clearly shows that the connection that exists between group-based culture and pronoun omission: Languages from cultures with a high group-based index score allow first-person pronouns to be omitted.

Language	Pronoun Omission?	Group-Based Culture Index Score
Arabic (Egypt)	yes	62
English (United States)	no	9
Finnish (Finland)	no	37
French (France)	no	29

51　pronoun: 代名詞
52　omit: 省く
53　correlation: 相関関係

German (Germany)	no	33
Greek (Greece)	yes	65
Japanese (Japan)	yes	54
Kikuyu (Kenya)	yes	73
Korean (South Korea)	yes	82
Mandarin (Taiwan)	yes	83

Table 6.5: The relationship between pronoun omission and a culture's individualist score

Kashima and Kashima hypothesize that the connection that exists between pronoun omission and group-based culture allows speakers to emphasize themselves, in contrast to the group, as required. Speakers can strategically[54] include the first-person pronoun when emphasis is required. Consider again the two example sentences. In comparison to the second sentence, the first sentence, 「私はご飯を食べた」, places much more emphasis on the speaker, and contrasts the speaker to the rest of the group. For example, imagine the scenario in which a mother arrives home from work late in the evening. She asks her two daughters if they have already eaten dinner. The older daughter has eaten, but the younger daughter has not. In this case, the sentence 「私はご飯を食べた」 is used by the older daughter to contrast herself with the younger daughter. What happens in English? Languages such as English must explicitly state the difference in order for the contrast to be communicated. For example, in this situation an English speaker must say "I have eaten, but sister has not."

Many differences exist between group-based cultures and non-grouped cultures. There are too many difference to discuss in this book. Table 6.6 summarizes the important differences presented in this book (see also Hofstede 2010: 113).

---

54 strategically: 戦略的に

Culturally Dependent Communication Styles

Group-Based Cultures	Non-Group-Based Cultures	Example from Book	Page
people introduce themselves as members of groups	people introduce themselves independent of the groups which they belong to	「もしもし、天満中学校、三年二組の山田太郎です」	115
the distinction between in-group and out-group is important	everyone is considered as an individual	parents of children from the same school greet each other	113
people avoid looking different from the group	being different and unique are considered as good qualities	an athlete denies an outstanding performance	116
high-context communication tends to be used more	low-context communication tends to be used more	(see discussion on context style communication in this chapter)	105, 109
the harmony of the group is maintained and arguments are avoided	speaking your own opinion is important and arguing is used to improve an idea	(see discussion of debate style in previous chapter)	80
the actions and behavior of one member of a group influence others in the group	people are more independent of the consequences of others actions	the academic performance of the students from 西江戸高等学校	118
pronoun use makes a distinction between the speaker and others in the group	people need to use several words to make a distinction between themselves and others	「私はご飯を食べた」	123

Table 6.6: The important differences that exist between group-based cultures and non-group-based cultures introduced in this book

Social power distance

The last topic discussed in this book is social power distance. Let's return for the last time to the character Bob. Here is another story about him.

In the previous stories about Bob, we learned that he is the president of an American-affiliated company in Tokyo. This company imports American food into Japan. At the time of this story, Bob is working hard to close a deal with a Japanese man named Suzuki. Suzuki-san inherited[55] the family business from his wife's father, Miyamoto-san, who recently retired. Miyamoto started the business when he was young, and grew it into a successful company. The company imports seafood for high-quality bento lunchboxes. Bob and Suzuki-san are closing[56] a deal to import crabs from the United States. They have met several times and things seemed to be progressing smoothly.

All of this changed one day when Bob was visiting Suzuki-san in his office, and Miyamoto-san suddenly showed up. The friendly and relaxed atmosphere in the office quickly became stiff[57] and formal. Bob was introduced to Miyamoto-san, and tea was served. Miyamoto-san began to complain about the horrible job his son-in-law[58] was doing as manager of the company. Bob disagreed, and praised Suzuki-san. Bob and Miyamoto-san also argued about the quality of American seafood. Bob thought that Miyamoto-san was very old-fashioned and too conservative[59]. Bob zealously[60] defended American seafood and carefully explained the techniques used to ensure high quality. During this conversation Suzuki-san remained quiet, but he began to look increasingly irritated[61]. However, Bob completely missed Suzuki's nonverbal

---

55　inherit: 受け継ぐ
56　close a deal: 契約を結ぶ
57　stiff: 改まった，堅苦しい
58　son-in-law: 義理の息子
59　conservative: 保守的な
60　zealously: 熱心に
61　irritated: 苛立つ

> messages.
>
> A few days later, Suzuki-san suddenly cancelled the business deal. When Bob pushed for an explanation, Bob was told that Suzuki had made a mistake and overestimated[62] the amount of food the company needed. Bob knew that this was not the truth. Furthermore, Bob could not understand why Suzuki-san would not tell him the real reason for the cancellation.

You should recognize some of the intercultural communication problems that Bob had. Bob did not know that criticizing the abilities of in-group members in Japanese culture is considered polite behavior (賀川洋 1997). Miyamoto criticized Suzuki's management of the company in order to appear modest[63] and polite. Bob also missed the high context style of communication of Suzuki (who became increasingly irritated). However, the biggest mistake that Bob made, and what probably destroyed the business deal, was arguing with Miyamoto. Not only do Japanese people tend to avoid arguing, but to argue with the founder[64] of the company was a very big mistake. In other words, Bob does not understand the importance of social power distance in Japanese culture.

In every society in the world, hierarchical relationships[65] exist. In these types of relationships, people higher in the hierarchy tend to have more power, prestige[66], wealth, and experience than people lower down in the hierarchy. For example, government leaders, company presidents, family heads, and army generals are located at the top of hierarchies, whereas part

---

62 overestimate: 多く見積もりすぎる
63 modest: 謙遜した，遠慮がちな
64 founder: 創設者
65 hierarchical relationship: 上下関係；hierarchy: 階級制
66 prestige: 威信

–time and temporary workers, new recruits[67], and newborn babies are located at the bottom of those hierarchies. One very important hierarchical relationship in Japanese society is the 先輩・後輩 relationship.

In many cultures of the world, great social distance exists between the people located at the top of the hierarchy and the people located at the bottom of the hierarchy. Because this social distance comes from differences in social power, it is called **social power distance**.

Because of social power distance, lower-ranking people show respect and politeness towards higher-ranking people. For example, Japanese people tend to avoid pointing out the mistakes of superiors[68] (Elwood 2001, 賀川洋 1997). Similarly, 後輩 tend to avoid disagreeing with 先輩. Social power distance is seen directly in the Japanese language itself as a complex system of 敬語. Not using the correct level of respect and politeness could be considered as rude. Going back to the story about Bob, we can see that he showed great disrespect towards Miyamoto by arguing with him. Then, Miyamoto later insisted that Suzuki end the business relationship with this rude foreigner. What should Bob have done in this situation? He should have agreed with Miyamoto, apologized for the seemingly poor quality of American seafood, and promised to do his best to sell only high quality seafood. Above all else[69], he should have taken care not to cause the founder of the company to lose face. Finally, Bob should have realized that Miyamoto is retired. Although everyone shows great respect and deference[70] towards him, in the end, Suzuki is now running the company and Suzuki makes the business decisions.

67　recruit: 新兵，入隊者
68　superior: 目上の人
69　above all else: 何よりも
70　deference: 敬意，服従

> **Check your understanding 6.5**
> The following are some of the ways that social power distance is expressed in Japanese society. Think of two more ways besides those listed here.
> - using polite language and standard language
> - the location of desks in an office (the boss's desk is located farthest away from the door)
> - avoiding criticism of a person who occupies a higher position within the same company
>
> *Answer: Two other ways that social power distance can be expressed are the cleaning up of sports equipment at the end of practice by the 後輩 members of a sports club, and the boss's use of harsh words in order to motivate a subordinate[71] (叱咤激励). There are many other possible answers in addition to these two.*

■ Social power distance and cultures around the world

Research on cultures around the world has shown that differences exist in the importance of social position and status in each culture. In some societies, very little social power distance is felt between people in different social positions. In other societies, social power distance is very large. The researchers that published the Group-Based Culture Index Scores listed in Table 6.4 also published a list of Social Power Distance Scores (Hofstede et al. 2010). A selection of these values, along with the Group-Based Culture Index Scores listed in Table 6.4, is presented in Table 6.7.

The Social Power Distance Scores indicate the extent to which social position is important, and the extent to which social power distance is felt

---

71 subordinate: 服従者，目下の人

between people. Indonesia has the largest index score, indicating that social power distance is very strong between people of different social positions. In contrast, in a country like Israel, social power distance is seldom felt.

Social power distance emerges in language in many different ways. In cultures that are sensitive to social power distance, titles of position and rank are very important. For example, Japanese culture uses titles such as 社長, お姉さん, 先輩, and 先生. In addition, important social practices are connected to names, and these practices determine when it is acceptable to call a person by a first name or by a nickname. In contrast, in cultures that are less sensitive to social power distance, the importance of these types of titles and distinctions is reduced. For example, in the Western countries, university students often call professors by their first names.

Culture	Group-Based Culture Index Score	Social Power Distance Index Score
United States	9	40
Canada	20	40
New Zealand	22	22
Italy	24	49
France	29	68
Finland	37	33
Israel	46	13
India	52	77
Japan	54	54
Arab countries	62	80
Philippines	68	94
Thailand	80	64
Korea	82	60
Taiwan	83	58
Indonesia	86	78

Table 6.7: Table 6.4 repeated along with each culture's Social Power Index Score

In cultures that a sensitive to social power distance, the opinions of people who possess authority[72] such as parents, doctors and teachers are believed to be correct. It would be very disrespectful for subordinates such as children, patients and students to disagree with the opinions of these more powerful individuals, at least in public. People in authority are expected to lead and subordinates are expected to follow without questioning their authority. In contrast, in societies that are not sensitive to social power distance, subordinates are expected to question and challenge the opinions of authority. Subordinates are also expected to provide their own opinion about leadership decisions. This occurs because, as I described in the section on debate style that appears in the previous chapter (page 80), in such cultures debating is considered to be a good way to improve an idea.

■ Connecting social power distance and group culture

Carefully examining Table 6.7 reveals a general relationship between Group-Based Culture Index Scores and Social Power Distance Index Scores:

> The more group-based a culture is, the more that culture tends to be sensitive to social power distance.

This relationship can clearly be seen in Figure 6.1, which is a scatter plot[73] that compares Group-Based Culture Index Scores with Social Power Distance Index Scores. Western cultures, such as the United States and Italy, are grouped together in the bottom-left corner of the plot. In general, Western cultures are not very sensitive to social power distance, and they tend to emphasize the individual over the group.

72　authority: 権威, 権力
73　scatter plot: 統計散布図

In contrast, Asian cultures, such as the Philippines and Taiwan, are grouped together in the top-right corner of the plot. These cultures are sensitive to social power distance, and they tend to emphasize the group over the individual. Note the location of Japan. It appears on the left edge of the Asian cultures, closest to the Western cultures. Over all, Japan is located in the center of the figure. This indicates that Japan is neither extremely group-based, nor extremely sensitive to social power distance.

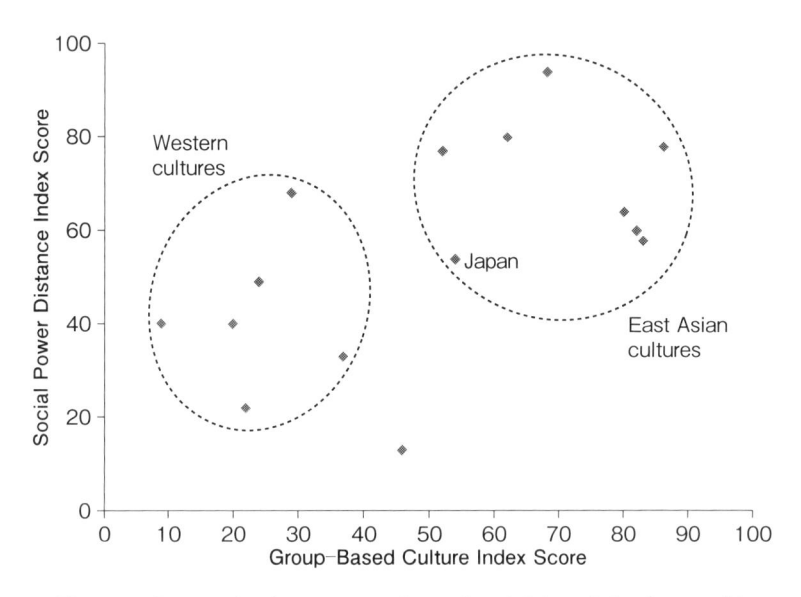

Figure 6.1: Scatter plot that compares Group-Based Culutre Index Scores with Social Power Index Scores

Check your understanding 6.6

In Figure 6.1, find the data point in the bottom center of the figure. Which country is represented by this data point? Based on the location of this data point in Figure 6.1, compare and contrast this country's culture with the culture of Japan.

Answer: Examining Table 6.4 shows us that the data point represents Israel. The Group-Based Cultural Index Score for Israel is almost the same as Japan, 46 versus 52. Thus, Israel is similar to Japan because both countries are moderately group-based. However, Israel and Japan differ greatly with respect to social power distance. In Japanese culture, the concept of social power distance is somewhat important. In contrast, the concept of social power distance is not at all important in Israeli culture.

Key points for Chapter 6

▶ The high context style of communication emphasizes using context to understand the nonverbal part of a message. In this style of communication, it is possible to say a specific message with vague[74] words, such as 「なんとかしてください」.
▶ The low context style of communication emphasizes the verbal component of a message. In this style of communication, a clear message is preferred and vague words are avoided.
▶ Many cultures of world, such as Japanese and Chinese cultures, prefer a high context style. Other cultures, such as English-speaking Western culture, prefer a low context style.
▶ Within every culture, there are situations that use a high context style and situations that use a low context style.
▶ In both a low context style of communication and debate style communication, clear explanations are important.
▶ In cultures that emphasize group style communication, group membership plays an important role in communication.
▶ Cultures that emphasize group style also tend to speak languages that allow pronoun omission.
▶ In cultures that emphasize social power distance, hierarchical relationships play an important role in communication.
▶ Cultures that emphasize group style communication also tend to emphasize social power distance.

---

74 vague: 曖昧な

Culturally Dependent Communication Styles

PRACTICE QUESTIONS

Q 6.1 The Asahi Brewery website[75] has both English versions and Japanese versions. At the top of each website is a motto[76]. The Japanese motto states, 「その感動を、わかちあう」. The English logo states, "Asahi aims to satisfy its customers with the highest levels of quality and integrity[77]." For each of these logos, decide if the logo is an example of low context communication of high context communication. Explain your choice. Does your answer match the claim that Western English-speaking cultures prefer a low context style of communication whereas Japanese culture prefers a high context style of communication?

Q 6.2 Because Japan is a group-based society, if one person in a group commits a crime, then others in the group may also be responsible for the crime. For each of the following situations, based on your own opinion, decide the extent to which you would be considered guilty of the crime. Choose among: guilty; somewhat guilty; somewhat innocent; and completely innocent.
- Your brother kills a man during a fight.
- You and the other members encourage a classmate to drink beer 「イッキ飲み」 at a circle party. The classmate later dies from alcohol poisoning[78].
- Your mother has a small car accident while you are with her in the car.

Q 6.3 For each of the following concepts, decide the communication style

---

75 Asahi: http://www.asahibeer.co.jp/.
76 motto: モットー, 標語
77 integrity: 誠実, 廉直
78 alcohol poisoning: アルコール中毒

to which it is connected (choose one of GROUP-BASED, NON-GROUP-BASED, and SOCIAL POWER DISTANCE). Then, decide if each of the following concepts is more important in Western culture or Japanese culture. The first one has been completed for you.

Concept	Communication Style	Culture
遠慮	group	Japanese
プライバシー		
同等関係		
上下関係		
わきまえ		
自立		
団体		
個性		
甘え		
ユニーク		
コネ		
好奇心		

Q 6.4 Here are two examples of cultural misunderstanding by Westerners living in Japan. For each example, perform the following. First, decide which communication style is being used by the Westerner, and which style is expected by Japanese culture. Second, write out some simple advice for the Westerners to help them understand Japanese culture better.

The JET programme （語学指導等を行う外国青年招致事業） recruits young university graduates to work in Japan as English teachers in schools. Many of these teachers do not have a good understanding of Japanese culture. Therefore, they sometimes experience culture shock and cultural miscommunication. One example of cultural miscommunication involves their attendance at the school. The issue related to days when classes are cancelled. There are many events throughout the school year such as 運動会 and 文化祭. Classes are cancelled for several days before these events to allow students to prepare and practice. During this time, although classes are cancelled, JET teachers are still expected to come to the school even though they have no work to do. Many JET teachers are angry that they must waste days doing nothing at the school.

This story is about a Canadian high school exchange student, Jeremy. Jeremy was 16 when he came to Japan. Thus, he was considered a first year high school student in Japan. He liked to play baseball, and joined the high school's baseball club. Although he was a first year student, he became good friends with one of the older students in the club, Tanaka. However, Jeremy had this habit of correcting Tanaka's English mistakes. This made Tanaka angry, and eventually they stopped being friends.

Q 6.5 In the past, Japan had a greater number of social rules, such as rules related to how to sit and how to laugh, than the number of rules seen today. This reduction in social rules suggests that modern Japanese culture differs greatly from medieval[79] Japanese culture with respect to the importance of the group and social power distance (Triandis 2006: 25). Approximately where do you think medieval Japan would be located on Figure 6.1? Explain your answer. Provide at least one concrete example of a social change that occurred

---

79 medieval: 中世の

between medieval Japan and modern Japan that supports your answer.

■ Final note

I hope that this book has made you more aware[1] of how you communicate, and more aware of cultural differences in communication. With this knowledge, you will have a positive experience communicating, not only with people from different cultures, but also with people from your own culture, such as members of the opposite sex. Communication is a skill, and, just like any other skill, with knowledge and practice, communication can be mastered. This type of mastery will become priceless in your daily and professional interactions with others, and it will be valuable for the rest of your life.

English References

Barnlund, Dean C. (1975). *Public and Private Self in Japan and the United States*. Tokyo: The Simul Press.
Bell, Allan. (1984). Language style as audience design. *Language in Society*, 13, 145-204.
Berlin, Brent and Paul Kay. (1969). *Basic Color Terms. Their Universality and Evolution. Berkeley*: University of California Press.
Copeland, Lennie and Lewis Griggs. (1986). *Going International: How to Make Friends and Deal Effectively in the Global Marketplace*. New York: New American Library.
Coupland, Nikolas. (1984). Accommodation at work: some phonological data and their implications. *International Journal of the Sociology of Language*, 46, 49-70.
Danesi, Marcel. (2008). *Language, Society, and Culture*. Toronto: Canadian Scholars' Press.
De Mente, Boyé. (2008). *Etiquette Guide to Japan*. Revised edition. Tokyo: Tuttle Publishing.
Elwood, Kate. (2001). *Getting Along with the Japanese*. Tokyo: Ask Co.
Geeraerts, Dirk. (2006). Prototype theory: Prospects and problems of prototype theory.

---

1 aware: 意識する

In Dirk Geeraerts (ed.) *Cognitive Linguistics: Basic Readings* (pp. 141-166). Berlin: Walter de Gruyter.

Giles, Howard and Philip Smith. (1979). Accommodation theory: Optimal levels of convergence. In Howard Giles and Robert N. St. Clair (eds.) *Language and Social Psychology* (pp. 45-65). Oxford: Blackwell.

Giles, Howard and Tania Ogay. (2007). Communication accommodation theory. In Bryan B. Whaley and Wendy Samter (eds.) *Explaining Communication: Contemporary Theories and Exemplars* (pp. 293-310). Mahwah, NJ: Lawrence Erlbaum.

Hofstede, Geert, Gert Jan Hofstede, and Michale Minkov. (2010). *Culture and Organaizations: Software of the Mind*. 3rd ed. London: McGraw Hill.

Hogan, Jackie. (2003). The social significance of English usage in Japan. *Japanese Studies*, 23, 43-58.

Hogg, Michael A. (2006). Social Identify Theory. In Peter J. Burke (ed.) *Contemporary Social Psychological Theories* (pp. 111-136). Stanford, CA: Stanford University Press.

Ip, Grace W. M., and Michael Harris Bond. (1995). Culture, values, and the spontaneous self-concept. *Asian Journal of Psychology*, 1, 30-36.

Kashima, Emiko S. and Yoshihisa Kashima. (1998). Culture and language: The case of cultural dimensions and personal pronoun use. *Journal of Cross-Cultural Psychology*, 29, 461-486.

Kraus, Michael W., Cassy Huang, and Dacher Keltner. (2010). Tactile communication, cooperation, and performance: An ethological study of the NBA. *Emotion*, 10, 745-749.

Nisbett, Richard E. (2006). Living together vs. going it alone. In Larry A. Samovar, Richard E. Porter and Edwin R. McDaniel (eds.) *Intercultural Communication* (pp. 103-113). 11th ed. Belmont: CA: Wadsworth.

Rosch, Eleanor. (1975). Cognitive representations of semantic categories. *Journal of Experimental Psychology*, 104, 192-233.

Russell, Bertrand. (1946/2004). *History of Western Philosophy*. London: Routledge.

Strange, Mary Z., Carol K. Oyster, and Jane E. Sloan. (2011). *Encyclopedia of Women in Today's World*. vol. 2. Los Angeles: Sage.

Tannen, Deborah. (1990). *You Just Don't Understand*. New York: Ballantine Books.

Tajfel, Henri and John C. Turner. (1979). An integrative theory of intergroup conflict.

In William G. Austin and Stephen Worchel (eds.) *The Social Psychology of Intergroup Relations* (pp. 33-47). Monterey, CA: Brooks/Cole.

Triandis, Harry C. (1994). *Culture and Social Behavior*. New York, NY: Mcgraw-Hill.

Triandis, Harry C. (2006). Culture and conflict. In Larry A. Samovar, Richard E. Porter and Edwin R. McDaniel (eds.) *Intercultural Communication* (pp. 22-31). 11th ed. Belmont: CA: Wadsworth.

Turner, John C. (1975). Social comparison and social identity: Some prospects for intergroup behavior. *European Journal of Social Psychology*, 5, 5-34.

Turner, John C., Rupert J. Brown and Henri Tajfel. (1979). Social comparison and group interest in in-group favoritism. *European Journal of Social Psychology*, 9, 187-204.

von Raffler-Engel, Walburga. (1996). Nonverbal communication. In Hans Goebl (ed.) *Contact Linguistics* (pp. 296-310). Berlin: Walter de Gruyter.

Wood, Julia T. and Christopher C. Inman. (1993). In a different mode: Masculine styles of communicating closeness. *Journal of Applied Communication Research*, 21, 279-295.

Wood, Julia T., and Nina M. Reich. (2006). Gendered communication styles. In Larry A. Samovar, Richard E. Porter and Edwin R. McDaniel (eds.) *Intercultural Communication* (pp. 177-186). 11th ed. Belmont: CA: Wadsworth.

Japanese References

賀川洋（1997）『誤解される日本人』講談社インターナショナル。
久米照元・長谷川典子（2007）『ケースで学ぶ異文化コミュニケーション』有斐閣選書。
東照二（2009）『社会言語学入門』（改訂版）研究社。
八代京子・荒木晶子・樋口容視子・山本志都・コミサロフ喜美（2001）『異文化コミュニケーションワークブック』三修社。

Kevin Heffernan（ケビン・ヘファナン）
関西学院大学総合政策学部准教授
1970年カナダ生まれ。1991年に交換留学生として初来日。トロント大学にて博士号（言語学）を取得。2009年より現職。研究分野は、外国語との言語接触の歴史、日本語の言語変化、欧米に居住する日本人の名前についてなど、幅広い範囲にわたる。

Introduction to Communication for Japanese Students
―大学生のためのコミュニケーション入門―

2013年4月24日　第1刷発行
2024年11月20日　第4刷発行

著者　　Kevin Heffernan

発行　　株式会社　くろしお出版
　　　　〒102-0084　東京都千代田区二番町4-3
　　　　電話：03-6261-2867　FAX：03-6261-2879　WEB：www.9640.jp

装丁　大坪佳正　　印刷所　シナノ書籍印刷

©2013 Kevin Heffernan, Printed in Japan
ISBN 978-4-87424-586-6 C1030
乱丁・落丁はおとりかえいたします。本書の無断転載・複製を禁じます。